Heritage of Care

Heritage of Care

The American Society for the Prevention of Cruelty to Animals

Marion S. Lane and Stephen L. Zawistowski

Foreword by Marty Becker, D.V.M.

PRAEGER

Westport, Connecticut
London

Library of Congress Cataloging-in-Publication Data

Lane, Marion.
    Heritage of care : the American Society for the Prevention of Cruelty to Animals /
Marion S. Lane and Stephen L. Zawistowski ; foreword by Marty Becker.
        p. cm.
    Includes bibliographical references and index.
    ISBN 978-0-275-99021-3 (alk. paper)
    1. American Society for the Prevention of Cruelty to Animals—History. 2. Animal
welfare—United States. 3. Bergh, Henry, 1811–1888. I. Zawistowski, Stephen. II.
Title.
    HV4702.L36 2008
    179′.306073—dc22   2007036176

British Library Cataloguing in Publication Data is available.

Library of Congress Catalog Card Number: 2007036176
ISBN: 978-0-275-99021-3

First published in 2008

Praeger Publishers, 88 Post Road West, Westport, CT 06881
An imprint of Greenwood Publishing Group, Inc.
www.praeger.com

Printed in the United States of America

The paper used in this book complies with the
Permanent Paper Standard issued by the National
Information Standards Organization (Z39.48-1984).

10 9 8 7 6 5 4 3 2 1

This book is dedicated to the ASPCA Board of Directors, past and present; members and supporters; and staff and volunteers who have kept Henry Bergh's vision alive for more than 140 years and maintained the ASPCA's "heritage of care."

Contents

Foreword

When Steve and Marion asked me to write the foreword for *Heritage of Care*, I had an immediate gut reaction—yes! Or rather—how could I not?

I've long supported the American Society for the Prevention of Cruelty to Animals (ASPCA). I've known several key players in the organization personally for more than three decades, and I've watched them stay true to their mission of "providing effective means of preventing cruelty to animals." The fact is, had Henry Bergh not founded the ASPCA in 1866—the first animal protection organization on this continent—the face of animal welfare would look very different today. It is this very "heritage of care," passed down by Bergh, that present-day ASPCA staff, members, and volunteers celebrate and pay homage to every day of their lives.

But this is much more than a history book on the nation's first animal welfare organization. It is an in-depth look at an organization founded by a man who was not particularly interested in animals—but who rose to protect them because it was the right thing to do. And it is this spirit of doing what is right and just, what is kind and humane, to not ignore but take action, that today's ASPCA staff continues to carry forward, just as Henry Bergh would have wanted them to do. Not because it's politically correct, or because it's fashionable, but because protecting animals—sentient beings who cannot speak for themselves—is simply the right thing to do.

Were Henry Bergh to visit the ASPCA today, I believe he would be proud to see what his simple action—halting the flogging of a cart horse—has wrought. Over the years, the organization has developed exceptional competencies in as wide a range of services as you can think of that relate to animal welfare. Today the ASPCA is synonymous with the protection of companion animals throughout the United States.

Although headquartered in Manhattan, the ASPCA has an extremely active Midwest office, which also happens to house the organization's Animal Poison Control Center and its Animal Behavior Center. Its National Outreach department and staff impact animals across the country through their hands-on work with shelter personnel in many communities. Its Anti-cruelty Initiatives and Training and Legislative Services departments draw attention to the inhumane treatment of animals nationwide, and lobby for legislation that will improve their lot.

Back home in Manhattan, the ASPCA's Pet Adoption Center, Bergh Memorial Animal Hospital, and Humane Law Enforcement department pool their expertise to provide for rescued animals, often taken from extremely abusive situations. Once considered the "dogcatcher" because it handled animal-control services for New York City for one hundred years, today the ASPCA's New York City services—which include a state-of-the art, limited-intake adoption facility—are a microcosm of its unique combination of core competencies, and serve as an urban model for other communities.

As a veterinarian, I know how instrumental the ASPCA was in shaping veterinary medicine in this country. The first horse ambulance was introduced by the ASPCA in 1867, before, even, a human ambulance. And as far back as 1877, Bergh recognized the critical absence of an accredited body to certify veterinarians. He brought French-trained Dr. Alexandre F. Liautard, the founder of the American Veterinary College in New York City in 1875, on board as an officer of the society. Because of the immense attention they paid to the quality of care received by the animals in their charge, Bergh and his associates at the ASPCA were credited with helping to elevate the veterinary profession by first engendering humane feelings toward animals—the roots of the animal advocacy that is so widespread today. And the ASPCA's animal hospital, which has seen more than one location in Manhattan, has always remained on the cutting edge of veterinary medicine. The society's in-house veterinary experts often lecture at major veterinary meetings, or are quoted in the media.

Heritage of Care will give you an insider's view into the competence, care, and compassion of one of the great organizations of our time, and one that has shaped society's attitude toward animals since the late nineteenth century. As the ASPCA continues its lifesaving work in the twenty-first century by helping to reshape entire communities as humane models, this book takes a fascinating look at the modern-day "Bergh's men and women" who are dedicated to keeping the "science and soul" of Henry Bergh's vision alive.

Dr. Marty Becker
Almost Heaven Ranch, Idaho
June 2007

Preface

I met Henry Bergh in 1988, one hundred years after his death. I had just begun to work at the ASPCA, and Bergh was living in a stack of boxes that were being stored in my basement office. Upon opening them, I found a collection of old annual reports, large scrapbooks of yellowed press clippings, Bergh's "letter books" in his own cursive hand, and myriad other documents that traced the then-120-year history of the ASPCA. I also found eight volumes of an unpublished and undated typescript with the title *Bergh's War on Vested Cruelty*, by Edward P. Buffet. Buffet, an early twentieth-century biographer and historian, had painstakingly researched these same materials to write the most exhaustive study in existence on the founder of the ASPCA. My coauthor and I are indebted to Buffet for our understanding of Bergh.

A variety of other artifacts from the society's long history were scattered around the building. They included the John Wood Dodge oil painting of Henry Bergh, the original petition signed by prominent New Yorkers calling for the formation of the society, old law-enforcement badges, and a photo here and another there with no story to explain them. But it was those boxes in my office that held the heart of the story. I began reading, and couldn't stop.

The ASPCA is like many nonprofit organizations. Its staff and directors are so busy going about the organization's mission that scant attention is paid to the history of the effort. Documents saved and preserved are often the result of happenstance and good fortune, rather than planned attention to history. Hundreds, if not thousands, of organizations are formed each year to pursue one laudable cause or another. It is rare, however, when one of these organizations goes on to stimulate a significant social movement. The ASPCA is one such organization. It now occupies a nether region betwixt history, myth, and a vibrant, modern organization.

The documents left for us are enthralling and frustrating. They tell a story of persistence and accomplishment. There are also gaps that leave us aching to know more about both the major achievements and the day-to-day activities during different eras. As the ASPCA readied itself to celebrate its 125th anniversary in 1991, I had the opportunity to interview a longtime employee who remembered helping to move the society in 1952 from the Lower East Side, where it had been situated for many years, to a new location on East 92nd Street and York Avenue. It was heartbreaking to hear that the urgency of the move resulted in many boxes of documents and other materials being discarded or lost. This knowledge made the contents of the boxes I found in the basement even more precious.

I am at heart a storyteller. And the ASPCA story is one that I've been trying to tell in one way or another for the past nineteen years. Many ASPCA staff have been in meetings with me when I've interjected an anecdote from the ASPCA's history. I've also incorporated these materials into lectures and publications on the history of the humane movement and animal shelters. This present volume is my first chance to tell a more complete story about the ASPCA. Marion Lane, who's been with the ASPCA for ten years, has been the perfect partner. We decided that we had neither the time nor training to write a scholarly history of the organization. We agreed that what we wanted to do was spin a yarn—tell a story that was both interesting and informative. It would also be as true as we could make it. An organization that is more than 140 years old will have had good times and bad times. We try to be honest in how we present these times. We have seen and experienced some of both.

In the end, we cannot help but be impressed with an organization that is refashioning itself to be relevant and effective in a third century. Most significant is the observation that over the past 140 years, the mission of the organization has been so compelling that it has attracted incredibly dedicated, intelligent, and hardworking staff, and remarkably generous members and supporters. It has endured, while many other organizations have not. It has not been defeated by changes in leadership, discontinuing some activities, and adding new ways of helping animals. In the end, the ASPCA's ability to meet challenges as they are presented is the best sign for its future. If the past is any guide, there's every indication that the society will continue to find new ways "to provide effective means for the prevention of cruelty to animals."

Stephen L. Zawistowski
June 2007

ASPCA Milestones

1866   The country's first animal welfare organization, The American Society for the Prevention of Cruelty to Animals® (ASPCA®), was founded by Henry Bergh. The society also prompted the New York State legislature to pass the country's first effective anticruelty law.

1867   Operated the first ambulance anywhere for injured horses—two years before New York's Bellevue Hospital put into service the first ambulance for humans.

1873   Promoted the mechanical "gyropigeon" as an alternative to live pigeon shoots.

1874   Bergh helped organize the first Society for the Prevention of Cruelty to Children (SPCC), following the rescue of an abused nine-year-old girl named Mary Ellen.

1875   Bergh invented a canvas sling for rescuing horses who got stuck in the mud or fell into the river.

1894   Assumed the job of caring for New York City's stray and unwanted animals, a function previously performed by New York City government.

1902   Put a motorized horse ambulance into service.

1912   Opened its first veterinary facility, a free horse dispensary.

1916   Started a formal education program for school children to promote the humane treatment of animals. Raised money to help care for the 934,000 horses who served in World War I.

1920   Advanced the use of anesthesia in animal surgery. First to use radium to treat cancer in animals.

1925   Began a weekly series of talks over the new communications medium: radio.

1928   Expanded the humane education program with classroom demonstrations in public schools and summer playgrounds.

1939   Inspected the 2,000 animals on exhibit at the New York World's Fair.

1942   Took wartime emergency measures and conducted courses on care of animals in the event of air raids.

1944   Inaugurated obedience-training classes for dogs and their owners.

1952   Began inspection of laboratories in New York that use animals for research—the first program of its kind in the country. These inspections arose from the passage of the Metcalf-Hatch Act, which required that animal shelters provide animals for research purposes.

1954   Expanded its animal hospital by adding a contagious-disease ward, pathology laboratory, X-ray therapy laboratory, and an internship program.

1958   Opened the Animalport at Kennedy International Airport to inspect and care for animals entering or leaving the country by plane. The ASPCA ran this facility until 1994.

1961   ASPCA hospital performed its first open-heart surgery on a dog.

1964   Acquired patents for pens for the humane slaughter of food animals and offered them royalty-free to meat packers throughout the world. Began a course to train animal handlers working for research institutions.

1966   Celebrated 100th anniversary by renaming the hospital after Henry Bergh and presenting a gold medallion to Walt Disney for his positive depiction of animals.

1973   Adoptions department began compulsory spay/neuter for all animals.

1976   Developed the "Bergh bandage" for orthopedic recovery.

1985   Government Affairs office opened in Washington, D.C.; department relocated to New York City following terrorist attacks of 2001.

1992   Began promoting the adoption of retired greyhounds, administering a grant from the American Greyhound Council to help rescue groups across the country.

1993   Along with nine other animal organizations, initiated National Council on Pet Population Study and Policy, and conducted the first survey and census of shelter animals in the United States.

1994   Helped to pass the 1994 New York State Animal Experimentation Bill that allows students who object to dissection to complete an alternative project without a negative impact on their grade.

1995   After 100 years of providing animal control services for New York City, the ASPCA declined to renew the contract in order to focus on national education, information, and advocacy.
Animated "Spokescritters" adopted by ASPCA from the Walt Disney animation studios began to appear in public service announcements.

1996   Acquired the National Animal Poison Control Center, the only veterinary toxicology telephone service operating 24 hours a day, 365 days a year. Inaugurated ASPCA Care-A-Van, a mobile spay/neuter clinic for the New York metropolitan area.

2000   First Henry Bergh Children's Book Awards recognize books based on exemplary handling of subject matter pertaining to animals and the environment.

2001   *Animal Precinct* launched on the Animal Planet network.

2001   Joined other local animal welfare agencies responding to World Trade Center attack. Cared for more than 500 animals within one week.

2004   Helped found Mayor's Alliance for New York City's Animals. ASPCA staff edited the first text on shelter medicine: *Animal Shelter Medicine for Veterinarians and Staff*.

2005   Pledged to make New York City a "no-kill" city in five years. Made lead grant of $5 million to Mayor's Alliance for NYC's Animals to further goal.
Deployed staff to Gulf Coast to assist in rescue and recovery following Hurricanes Katrina and Rita. Gave more than $13 million in grants to shelters and organizations in the region.

2006   Unveiled new state-of-the-art vertical urban shelter for 140th anniversary.

2007   Launched ASPCA Mission: Orange™ to create humane communities in Austin, Philadelphia, Tampa, Gulfport-Biloxi, and Spokane.

Chapter 1

"The Great Meddler"

Henry Bergh was not an animal lover. That he nevertheless took on the thankless task of preventing cruel treatment of "the brute creation" in America—at a time when slaves had only just gained their freedom and women were still sixty years away from the right to vote—comes as a surprise to many. For what could otherwise impel the proud, pampered, and protected heir to a sizeable fortune to give up his comfort and leisure to pursue a cause that exposed him variously to scorching heat, numbing cold, and scenes of unimagined brutality, not to mention scorn, ridicule, and the odd threat of assassination?

"I was never specially interested in animals," Bergh told a reporter for the *New York Mail and Express* in June 1884, nearly two decades after he founded the American Society for the Prevention of Cruelty to Animals, the first animal-protection organization in North America. The interview took place in Bergh's office at the society's second home, a "pretty building" at Fourth Avenue and Twenty-second Street in New York City. "I always had a natural feeling of tenderness for creatures that suffer," Bergh explained, "but what struck me most forcibly was that we were deriving such immense benefits from these creatures and gave them in return not the least protection." In one word, what motivated Henry Bergh was injustice. And although his tender feelings toward suffering creatures dated back to his youth, when he is reputed to have fought with boys intent on drowning stray dogs and cats in the East River, Bergh as animal advocate was a late bloomer. He was a full fifty years of age—and those are nineteenth century years—before he figured out what he wanted to be when he grew up.

The American nation, not even thirty years old, was at war with England when Henry Bergh was born in New York City. The date was August 29, 1813. Henry, the youngest child of Elizabeth and Christian

Bergh, grew up with his brother Edwin and sister Jane in a modest, two-story home on the Lower East Side of Manhattan—then, as Bergh described it, a "fashionable and respectable locality," with a nearby orchard and white sandy beach on the East River where Henry swam as a boy. Within a few short decades the neighborhood would teem with successive waves of poor immigrants from Ireland, the European continent, and China, attracted by the prospect of work in the rapidly industrializing big American city. A scant twenty blocks from Bergh's childhood home was the district called Five Points, which in the same few decades would become the infamous slum so vividly depicted in the 2002 Academy Award–nominated film, *Gangs of New York*.

Whatever hardships it brought, the War of 1812 was good for the shipbuilding business. Two years before the war, Bergh's father, a hard-working and exacting marine architect, had opened his own shipyard at Corlears Hook on the East River. Because of Christian's previous success in building a frigate for the U.S. Navy, he was called upon to construct a number of vessels for the American fleet. By the time he retired in 1837, Christian Bergh had not only contributed importantly to advances in the design and speed of transatlantic craft, but had also amassed a fortune. In an unpublished article about his father's life, Henry Bergh wrote that the elder Bergh had spent the years from 1812 to 1815 on Lake Ontario, building ships for the Navy. A twenty-first century perspective suggests that his father's absence during Henry's earliest years surely would have had an impact on the young boy's development. What we do know is that while Henry wrote with great pride of his father's accomplishments in the world, it was his mother's influence that he acknowledged in forming his compassionate nature, commenting once that most of what was good in him, he owed to her. To a *Philadelphia Press* reporter he once commented, "I don't suppose I would ever have undertaken this work unless fate had cursed me with a very sensitive nature easily moved at the spectacle of cruelty or injustice." Additional evidence that Bergh possessed heightened sensitivities can be found in the reports that he dyed his hair and steadfastly refused to say how old he was. On the latter sub-ject, the most he would ever admit to was "fifty, and upwards." The early-twentieth-century historian and author, Edward P. Buffet, who wrote an unpublished biography of Bergh, explains Henry's misrepresen-tation about his age this way: "The lateness when he began his true life work no doubt sharpened his soreness upon his senility."

What Henry Bergh did owe his father, in addition to his inheritance and his height—both were taller than six feet at a time when the average height for American men was five feet six inches—was his powerful sense of purpose. In recalling Christian's contribution to the shipbuilding industry, Henry may just as well have been describing his own labors in the field of animal protection:

Naturally endowed with a refined taste and an inventive genius, combined with untiring industry, he applied his whole efforts to the advancement of his profession with a devotion and singleness of purpose rarely if ever, equaled. [I] was informed by him that he had not been able to find an opportunity in the space of forty years to gratify his inclination to visit the scenes of his youthful days.

When Henry settled on his life's work, however belatedly, he pursued it to the exclusion of all else.

From both parents, Bergh received memorable lessons in the importance of being honest. His father imparted an abhorrence of indebtedness, and his mother the virtue of never taking anything that didn't belong to him—up to and including a coin found in the street. These traits would become key in Bergh's role as head of the ASPCA.

Three other characteristics, completely unrelated, which would figure importantly in Bergh's success as a champion of the animal cause, were (1) a penchant for writing, (2) a tendency toward autocracy, and (3) an uncommon degree of courage. The first allowed Bergh, in an age before radio, television, and the Internet, to keep his cause constantly before the public through articles and especially letters in New York's many newspapers. The second—his tendency toward autocracy—figured significantly in discovering his passion for compelling others to treat animals kindly, and subsequently in leading the ASPCA successfully through its first two decades. Thirdly, his courage permitted him to pursue justice for animals wherever abuse of them led: to the muddy streets, the docks, the slaughterhouses, the dogfighting pits, and the country estates where sporting gentlemen practiced their marksmanship on pigeons and where hare were coursed by purebred hounds.

Few particulars are known about Henry Bergh's interests and activities as a boy and young man. He matriculated in the class of 1834 at Columbia College, but left before graduating. In 1835, at the age of twenty-two, he joined his father in C. Bergh and Co., the family shipbuilding business. When Christian retired two years later, Henry and his brother Edwin reorganized the business as Bergh & Co.

Shipbuilding in New York was beginning to decline, however, and around the time of Christian's death in 1843, the yard was closed. Thus ended Henry Bergh's stint as an industrialist and businessman. How it suited him, or he it, is uncertain, but it is reasonable to assume that he gained from this experience a solid understanding of the fundamentals of running a business, especially considering his father's reputation as the "honestest man in New York." Any number of his father's hard-nosed practices would become evident in the way that Bergh managed the ASPCA a quarter-century later. The one he seemed most adamant about—surely instilled in him by his father—was that the society should never be in debt.

In 1839, at age twenty-six, Bergh married Catharine Matilda Taylor, the tall, beautiful, and accomplished daughter of an English gentleman who had immigrated to New York. Although a wedding was planned at the historic St. Mark's Episcopal Church, which originated in 1660 as a chapel built by Peter Stuyvesant, for reasons unknown the couple eloped instead. Nevertheless, it was at St. Mark's—today a thriving community church and designated historic New York City landmark—that both Matilda and Henry's funeral services later would be held, and both were buried in Brooklyn's Green-Wood Cemetery, the final resting place of scores of New York's most prominent citizens. In May 2006, a public event commemorating the ASPCA's 140th anniversary was held at Green-Wood, and a two-month-long exhibit, "Blessed Are the Merciful: Celebrating Henry Bergh and the ASPCA," opened in the cemetery's chapel. Hundreds of New Yorkers marked the occasion. To honor Henry Bergh, Green-Wood welcomed select animals into the cemetery for the first time in its 168-year history.

In his thirties and forties, Henry Bergh lived the life of a wealthy socialite. His inheritance was estimated as "a large fortune," and Henry and Matilda were soon appearing at fashionable parties and balls in New York, Saratoga Springs, and Washington, D.C., where the handsome couple frequently attracted favorable comment in local papers. In 1847 the Berghs, who had no children, sailed to Europe for the first of many extended trips. This time they stayed for three years and visited France, Spain, Germany, Austria, Greece, Turkey, Egypt, Italy, Switzerland, England, and Scotland. In the fashion of the time, Henry kept detailed diaries of their travels, noting where they went, whom they met, what they saw and did, even what they ate and drank—as well as their impressions. These diaries, in Bergh's accomplished handwriting, have been preserved in the archives of the ASPCA, and in some entries there are hints at things to come. For example, while traveling in Spain in 1848, Henry and Matilda attended several bullfights, including one at which eight bulls were killed and twenty horses gored to death as the spectators, including ladies, roared their approval. In his diary, Bergh noted, "Never before has a similar degree of disgust been experienced by us, or such hearty contempt for a people calling themselves civilized and at the same time Christians."

Bergh never lost his sense of disgust at the "wicked butchery" of the bullfight. Thus when a Spanish matador attempted to introduce bullfighting to New York City in 1881, some thirty-three years later, ASPCA President Bergh sprang into action. The state's existing anticruelty law prohibited such a contest, and Bergh showed up at the makeshift arena on 116th Street with seventy police officers and several of his own agents to make sure the law was enforced.

It was! Three thousand persons had paid admittance to watch the bloody spectacle, but since no blood was shed, the spectators entertained themselves by ridiculing the event. On the second day of the exhibition, attendance numbered only about two dozen, and then a fortuitous cloudburst washed away all traces of the failed enterprise. Bergh reported on this event in the society's fifteenth annual report. It surely was a personal triumph for the former traveler who had been so dismayed by Spain's depravity. However, if Spain knew of Bergh's "disgust and contempt," it gave no indication of caring. It would be another 123 years before Spain made the first serious move to break with its cruel tradition. In 2004, the city council of Barcelona voted to ban bullfights. It was the first municipality in Spain to do so.

During his forties, Bergh pursued what appears to have been his first career choice: that of playwright. Live theater in New York City had gotten off to a slow start—theatrical performances were prohibited under Dutch rule in the seventeenth century—but by Bergh's time, interest was surging, and a rapidly growing number of theaters offered everything from minstrels and animal acts to melodramas, morality plays, operas, and Shakespeare. Bergh wrote a number of farces that he was occasionally able to persuade a theater manager to produce. The reviews were lukewarm at best, sometimes much worse. The most common complaint was that the would-be satirist lacked a sense of humor. Bergh also wrote poetry, which likewise found no favor. Once he had become noted for his work in animal protection, contemporaries who reflected on his earlier literary efforts felt that the subject matter was unworthy of the great humanitarian.

Broadway's loss was the brute creation's gain. The unappreciated poet and dramatist found ample outlet to colorfully express his point of view in the letters pages of New York City's dozen or so daily newspapers. In this pursuit, Bergh did not restrict himself to the facts. While rational argument was the mainstay of his communications, he brought every ounce of wit and erudition at his command to bear on the subjects to which he put his pen. Phrases in French and Latin were used liberally. A line of poetry might be quoted. The result was both scathing and entertaining, while at the same time proper, formal, and technically correct. For example, in an attempt to persuade the city *not* to build a park in the Corlears Hook area where he grew up, Bergh wrote to a legislator in 1883:

Myself and family are the unfortunate owners of much property there, and I have often intreated the Tax Commissioners to take it off my hands at less than they say it is worth, but while the intellectual standards of our officials is not too high, those gentlemen are not such idiots as to accept my proposal. There probably exists, in that eastern angle of the city, a larger crop of thieves and other vagabonds than can be found anywhere in this state—Hunters Point always excepted.

It is now proposed to provide that criminal population with a park, or place of rendezvous, where they can mature their depredations—while they sit, and sun, and scratch themselves.

In spite of Bergh, the park was built, although not until after his death. Corlears Hook Park still exists today. The four-acre site is located along what was designated in the mid-twentieth century as the Atlantic Flyway. Ironically, the proposed "place of rendezvous" for thieves and vagabonds that Bergh decried provides a green space where migratory birds can rest and refuel—and be appreciated by twenty-first-century nature lovers.

Early on, Bergh's father's political connections, and his own and his wife's social station, no doubt made it easy for editors to accept Bergh's unsolicited views on the broad variety of subjects that interested him. Once he had founded the ASPCA, however, Bergh himself became news. Thereafter, a large part of the struggle to educate the public on humane issues, as well as to publicize those who were helping or harming the cause, was waged in the press. It would be impossible to underestimate the value of free publicity to the promulgation of humane attitudes in America, and a very large part of the credit goes to Henry Bergh's astute use of the medium. Had his playwriting and other literary efforts met with approbation, who knows if he would have had the same amount of time and energy for letter writing? Though never the "man of letters" he wanted to be, he was very much a man of "letters."

Bergh's correspondence in the cause of preventing cruelty was prodigious. Letters to newspaper editors comprised only a small part. In addition, he wrote to politicians and legislators to argue his point of view, to judges and magistrates and chiefs of police to take them to task. To canal companies, shipping companies, and the heads of railroads (even those named Vanderbilt), he wrote to complain about the cruel treatment of animals, as he did to rabbis who oversaw kosher slaughterhouses. He responded graciously and at length to animal advocates in other parts of the state, country, and world who sought his advice on forming "branch" societies. He wrote to wealthy benefactors who donated large sums to the society, and to ordinary citizens who sent him a dollar to further the work.

Bergh wrote his own correspondence. Whether this practice was acquired while working for his father is not known, but may be suspected. In 1883 Bergh wrote to the Hon. Franklin Edson, newly elected mayor of New York City. A day or two later, he received a reply from the mayor's secretary. This slight prompted Bergh to make this comment in his reply:

The undersigned would … avail himself of the occasion to remind the Secretary of His Honor that his communication was not addressed to him—however worthy a gentleman he may be—but to the Mayor of the City of New York.

Times seem to be greatly changed since he was a boy, when the Mayor of his Native City assumed none of the attributes of Royalty but in a democratic-republican fashion, responded personally to any useful and respectable citizen, and not by deputy.

If Bergh seems to have overreacted, it's important to remember that Americans who grew up within family memory of the War of Independence were slow to recover any level of comfort with the slightest appearance of entitlements based on class. After all, George Washington agreed to serve as first *president* of the new American nation, not as first king.

For the twenty-two years that Henry Bergh presided over his society, he pointed proudly to its growth and the spread of its influence. At the end of the society's twentieth year, Bergh noted with satisfaction that the number of members stood at slightly more than 500. In 2007, membership had risen to more than 800,000. Bergh surely would be delighted to see the society's progress. But even he would be hard-pressed to personally answer that much mail.

While in Europe, and again back in the States, where they spent at least one winter in Washington, D.C., the Berghs were frequently seen in the company of those at the pinnacle of political power and cultural prominence. Meanwhile, a subsequent trip abroad took Henry and Matilda to "the Orient," including Russia—which Henry found very much to his liking. In due course he began to entertain the idea of a career in foreign service, which in hindsight seems a natural choice. During the administration of President James Buchanan, there was some speculation in the press that Bergh was under consideration for a diplomatic position in Russia—where Buchanan had previously served as minister. Nothing came of the rumor, however, until Abraham Lincoln was in office and William Seward—a resident of Bergh's home state of New York who had himself served in Russia—was secretary of state. In May 1863, Bergh was appointed secretary of the American Legation in St. Petersburg. Biographer Buffet sums up the perfect marriage of person and position:

His long residence in foreign capitals and recently in Russia itself, his familiarity with the customs of the aristocracy, his strong support of the Northern side in the war, were reasons which might have been considered ample at that critical time, even had he lacked social and political influence at home. His personal bearing was such as would be recognized with respect anywhere, his private means were large, and the rare felicity of expression which his letters, if not his poems and dramas show, rendered him unusually well fitted to conduct the delicate diplomatic correspondence which would fall to him. To these personal qualities we may attribute the marked favors which he was destined to receive from the Emperor.

Thus as Henry and Matilda sailed from New York in early June of 1863, a scant two months before Henry's fiftieth birthday, it seemed that Bergh might at last find his calling. And so he would—but it was not to be diplomacy.

At first Henry Bergh's new job suited him well. Writing home after just a few weeks, he said, "I am thoroughly at work in my official position and like it amazingly. In short it is, of all other occupations, the one best adapted to my ambition and tastes. I believe I could make my mark in it if allowed to remain long enough, and in the position of minister." Bergh was already speculating that his next assignment might be Belgium or Italy. Then something happened to change his mind....

The year is 1863, the place Imperial Russia. Tsar Alexander II is on the throne. No one knows it yet, but two hundred years of rule by the Romanov dynasty is wending inexorably toward the Russian Revolution. As much as in any place on earth, the contrast between the power and wealth of the ruling class and the poverty and ignorance at the bottom of society, is striking. The Industrial Revolution that is rapidly changing the face and pace of Bergh's hometown has barely begun to take hold in this most undeveloped of the world's major powers. On the other hand, it would be hard to find a more opulent or tradition-drenched society than the court of Alexander II. Only two years earlier the tsar emancipated some twenty million serfs, but this act had yet to bring discernible change in Russian society. Generations of fealty and obeisance to a tsar do not evaporate overnight.

Henry Bergh, accompanied by his wife, is making a social call. His long, lean physique is folded carefully into the elegant carriage of the U.S. minister. The Russian coachman assigned to him is resplendent in the livery of the diplomatic corps. Legation Secretary Bergh is deep in thought as the carriage rolls along a fashionable avenue in St. Petersburg. As the carriage slows to turn up a side street, Bergh's meditation is interrupted by angry shouts. Through the coach window, Bergh sees that a droshky is stopped at the opposite side of the road, the horse in harness refusing to put weight on his right foreleg. The driver is standing at the horse's head, yanking angrily on the bridle. He raises one arm and begins beating the animal on the neck with a heavy stick. Blows fall again, and again, and again. The terrified animal tries to pull away, incurring the renewed wrath of the driver.

Bergh hesitates—then calls to his coachman, with whom he is able to converse in French.

"Ask that man to stop beating his horse," Bergh says. "Can't he see the poor brute is injured?"

The coachman turns in disbelief. "Monsieur?"

"Insist that he cease at once," Bergh says more sharply.

The coachman, unused to questioning authority, does as he's told. The droshky driver, even more unused to arguing with gentlemen, immediately puts aside his stick.

Bergh sits back against the cushions, half elated, half amazed. In that instant the course of history is redirected. Recalling the incident later, Bergh commented that at last he had found a way to utilize his gold lace, "and about the best use that can be made of it."

From all reports, Bergh received high marks for his performance as secretary, both within the legation and in Washington, D.C. He also was a favorite of the tsar, who on one occasion made his private yacht available for the American's use. Thus it came as a surprise to all when Bergh resigned his position after little more than a year of service, citing "the severity of the climate." It was true that Bergh was susceptible to respiratory infections—he attributed these to having nearly drowned not once but twice—but if the climate were the only factor, as Buffet points out, why not ask to be reassigned somewhere less severe?

With no definitive answers to discourage speculation, it's tempting to conclude that Bergh experienced an epiphany in the embassy coach, suddenly seeing the effect he could have in the world and how good it felt to make a difference. There is enough evidence of his didactic nature to support this notion: that it would not take much to set his foot upon a path whereon he might be able to compel others to behave as he believed they should—in this case, to treat their beasts of burden with kindness. "Oh, for a brief reign of autocracy!" he once confided to a friend when they were discussing the ignorance and brutality of horse drivers in New York. The friend played dumb and asked who might be entrusted with such power. "Who? Who?" Bergh cried. "I know of but one man—Henry Bergh!"

The epiphany theory is not without merit. Bergh himself, at least in later years, readily credited his experiences in Russia with his decision to try to find a way to improve the lot of animals. He consistently told reporters that a sound scolding by his officially attired Russian coachman was often enough to stop droshky drivers from abusing their horses. "Encouraged by my success," he said, "I made up my mind that when I came home I would prosecute those who persecuted poor dumb brutes and would try to compel justice to the lower animals from whom man derives two-thirds of the benefits he enjoys."

Having resigned his diplomatic post, Henry returned to the United States by way of England, where he and Matilda stopped for several months. The Society for the Prevention of Cruelty to Animals had been founded in London in 1824. When it subsequently gained the patronage of Queen Victoria, the name was changed to the Royal Society for the Prevention of Cruelty to Animals. The president of the RSPCA when Bergh visited in 1865 was the Earl of Harrowby, and its secretary was Mr. John Colam. These gentlemen were generous with their time and counsel, and Bergh never hesitated to acknowledge his indebtedness to English precedents for the form, character, bylaws, methodology, and even the name of his own American society. In the ASPCA's first annual report, and for years thereafter, the Earl of Harrowby and John Colam were listed as members ex officio.

Bergh was already well versed on animal issues by the time of his London visit. In 1863, despite the American press's preoccupation with the Civil War, at least one reporter wrote graphically and at length about the mistreatment of animals in New York City. A copy of an article titled "Cruelty to Animals" was pasted into Bergh's "Russian Scrapbook." It proves that Bergh not only was aware of the abuses that were taking place in his native land, but was also assembling information on the subject.

Also in Bergh's possession, seemingly from the mid-1850s, was a scrapbook of newspaper clippings and other printed materials on humane issues that dated back to the years 1824 to 1826 in Ireland and England. The scrapbook traced the evolution of the humane cause in those countries. Buffet calls the scrapbook "a text-book of [Bergh's] humane education." One individual who figured prominently in the scrapbook was Member of Parliament Richard Martin of Galway—nicknamed "Humanity Martin"—who achieved passage in 1822 of the first British act to protect animals from cruelty, and who helped to found the RSPCA. With a law in place, Martin set about enforcing it himself, accosting offenders on the streets of London and bringing them before local magistrates for prosecution and sentencing. An article from the *Liverpool Mercury* of April 8, 1825, makes it clear that Martin had recently been ridiculed in London's *Morning Chronicle*, the first newspaper to report on the sessions of Parliament. Clearly Bergh identified with Richard Martin, later working the streets in person as Martin had, even anticipating the ridicule that he, in turn, would suffer in the American press. "Before undertaking this labor," he wrote years later, "I took a careful survey of all the consequences to me personally—and I recognized the fact that I should be much abused, and ridiculed, and hence it was necessary for me to forget myself completely." Prophetic words! When Bergh began to interfere with individuals—and businesses—that were mistreating animals in New York City, he was dubbed not "Humanity Henry," which he might have relished, but "The Great Meddler," an unkind play on Lincoln's famous epithet, "The Great Emancipator," so familiar to everyone at the time.

If Henry Bergh seems an unlikely champion of the humane cause in America, the cause itself was inevitable. Reform was in the air, and the postwar boom had created new wealth and new recruits to social causes.

The rapidly expanding labor market that accompanied industrialization in America led to floods of immigrants, which in turn led to crowding, public health and sanitation issues, and a crying need for services to help the growing numbers of homeless and poor women and especially children. The war effort in the North, not to mention the influx of recently freed blacks, compounded the opportunities and the problems. With automobiles, electrified rail and trolley lines still decades in the future, horse power was the only mode of transportation both of people and of goods, and the misuse, overuse, and frank abuse of horses in New York City took place in full view of the public, perhaps for the first time and certainly on an unprecedented scale. At the same time, the ever-increasing volume of livestock being shipped by rail into the city from points west created a new and appalling spectacle of disease and suffering.

The fact that draft animals and food animals alike were suffering in full view of the public and especially of children was a significant point in the anticruelty argument in 1866. Leading thinkers of the day may not have agreed on the brute creation's right to kind treatment, but they very likely were agreed on the negative impact that witnessing cruel behavior could have on the moral development of children. Likewise, those who may have wanted biblical backup before acknowledging that animals were entitled to either mercy or justice, were less ambivalent about the harm done to the perpetrators themselves through their acts of animal cruelty. In general, it was easier to make a case for kindness on the basis of a cruel act's effect on human beings than on animal victims. But to give the devil his due, it's important to remember that in 1866 it had not yet been widely acknowledged that animals had even the capacity to feel pain.

For nearly two hundred years, the theories of the seventeenth century French philosopher René Descartes had held sway, including his view that nonhuman animals were no more than machines—complex and organic, but machines nonetheless. In Bergh's day, Descartes' views were finally giving way to the thinking of eighteenth century English philosopher Jeremy Bentham, who famously observed that it was not animals' ability to think, or to talk, that gave them the right to their own portion of happiness on earth, but their ability to suffer. Bentham, sometimes called the father of animal rights, was not particularly interested in animals, either. In his view, all members of society—women, children, mentally handicapped persons, slaves, homosexuals, *and* animals—had an equal right to not be caused to suffer.

And so mid-nineteenth century America saw ideas, events, and individuals come together and fuel a fervor for societal reform, most notably expressed in opposition to slavery but also passionate about rights for women and protections for animals and children. As different as the victim classes and issues were, the reform movements were similar in recognizing the rights of previously disenfranchised groups. In New York City, as word spread of Henry Bergh's crusade to protect animals from abuse, a social worker appealed to him to intervene in the case of an abused child. He agreed, explaining that a helpless child and a dumb animal were equally deserving of his help. "Both are God's creatures," he wrote. "Neither can protect themselves. My duty is imperative to aid them." Aid them he did. Eight years after founding the American Society for the Prevention of Cruelty to Animals, Henry Bergh cofounded the Society for the Prevention of Cruelty to Children—also the first association of its kind in America.

At the conclusion of his stay in England in 1865, there was nothing left but for Bergh to go home and start protecting animals. In this he would need tremendous courage. The dapper gentleman would have to get his hands dirty. He would have to swallow his pride and ask strangers for money and support. He would sacrifice his health and comfort, as well as the friendship of other gentlemen in his social circle when he challenged their hunting and horseracing interests. When he was, as he predicted, vilified and ridiculed in the press, he had to remain steadfast. In Russia, which had no anticruelty law, Bergh discovered that good intentions and gold lace were all he needed to curb the mistreatment of animals. In America, he would need to found a society, get a law passed, and win the power to enforce it. And then the real work would begin.

Chapter 2

The Work Begins

On the evening of February 8, 1866, a winter storm raged across New York City. It was a night not fit for man or beast, yet inside the Mercantile Library in Clinton Hall on Astor Place, 53-year-old Henry Bergh prepared to address the members of the American Geographical and Statistical Society. In his patrician hands he held the text of his talk, "Statistics Related to the Cruelties Practiced on Animals." Despite the tempest that swirled along the city's cobblestoned streets, the event was well attended. Three weeks earlier a printed circular had announced Bergh's lecture and its purpose: to establish a society "kindred to that so long in successful operation in London."

Bergh had left nothing to chance. Before addressing the public at Clinton Hall, he personally had contacted dozens of New York City's most influential citizens to solicit their support for his idea. He had written out the following brief statement of intent to found a society to prevent cruelty to animals and asked those who agreed with its mission to sign on as patrons:

The undersigned, sensible of the cruelties inflicted upon Dumb Animals by thoughtless and inhuman persons; and desirous of suppressing the same—alike from considerations affecting the moral well being of society, as well as mercy to the brute creation: consent to become patrons of a Society having in view the realization of these objects.

Bergh considered these scant fifty words to be nothing less than a declaration of independence for animals, and he believed that eventually the document would be held "in almost as much veneration" as the one drafted by Thomas Jefferson in 1776.

The individuals who signed the declaration were movers and shakers in the life of the city, state, and nation. Bergh was careful to recruit people with the means, influence, and visibility to help his new organization succeed. Among them:

- Politicians John T. Hoffman, mayor of New York City, who would later become governor; A. Oakey Hall, New York County Attorney, who would succeed Hoffman as mayor; John A. Dix, governor of New York, U.S. senator and secretary of the treasury under President Buchanan, also a famous Civil War general (Fort Dix, New Jersey, is named for him); Hamilton Fish, likewise a New York State governor and U.S. senator, subsequently tapped by President Grant as secretary of state.
- Financier and thoroughbred-racing enthusiast August Belmont, for whom the Belmont Stakes, initiated in 1867 and today the third leg in racing's Triple Crown, is named.
- "Merchant prince" Alexander T. Stewart, proprietor of the world's first department store.
- George Talbot Olyphant, president of the Delaware & Hudson Canal Company.
- Industrialist Peter Cooper, who founded Cooper Union, the nation's first "free" institution of higher learning in architecture, engineering, and the arts.
- John Jacob Astor Jr., heir to the real estate tycoon for whom Astor Place, the Astor Library (now the Joseph Papp Public Theater), and indeed Astoria, a neighborhood in Queens, are named.
- The renowned publishing enterprise of Harper & Brothers; journalists Frank Leslie (*Frank Leslie's Illustrated Newspaper*); Moses Beach (*The Sun*); Horace Greeley (*New York Tribune*), for whom Greeley Square is named; and poet William Cullen Bryant (*New York Review and Athenaeum Magazine*), in whose honor Bryant Park still stands.
- Philanthropists James Lenox, founder of Columbia Presbyterian Hospital and the Lenox Library; William H. Aspinwall, railroad and steamship company owner who helped found the Metropolitan Museum of Art.
- Clergymen—most notably the Right Reverend Horatio Potter, bishop of the Protestant Episcopal Church, and His Eminence, Archbishop John McCloskey, the first American cardinal.

To be sure, not all of the individuals who signed Bergh's declaration were destined to have New York City institutions as namesakes. Nevertheless, they were important people for Bergh to have on his side. Included in the number of less prominent individuals who signed on as patrons of the society were Thomas C. Acton, Metropolitan Police Board president (analogous to today's police commissioner); William McMurray, treasurer of the Metropolitan Police; John A. Kennedy, a police superintendent who nearly lost his life in the Draft Riots of 1863; several police inspectors, and at least one member of the city judiciary. Bergh knew he would need allies in enforcing the animal-cruelty law as well as in handing down sentences to those who broke it. In the end, despite poor weather and competing claims on their time, some two dozen of the men who signed Bergh's declaration of independence for animals attended the Clinton Hall lecture.

In 1966, the ASPCA marked its one-hundredth anniversary with a special publication called *The ASPCA Story*. To reprise the list of distinguished New Yorkers who supported the ASPCA at its founding, a 100-member "salute committee" of prominent twentieth-century citizens of the city was printed in the booklet. Among them were a dozen descendants of the society's original list of patrons.

The particulars of Bergh's Clinton Hall talk—certainly one of the first on animal welfare in the United States—appeared in the next day's papers. Bergh had begun by explaining that he felt compelled to found a society to prevent cruelty to the "mute servants of mankind," creatures that the Most High had committed to the care and mercy of human beings. He then catalogued the more egregious "inhuman" practices involving animals from ancient to modern times: the bloody spectacles of the Roman arena, so similar to the bullfights he had attended in Spain in the demoralizing effect they had on spectators; the vivisectionists in Paris, who dissected living dogs and horses, several operating simultaneously on different parts of one fully conscious animal (the use of anesthetic agents in veterinary medicine, although introduced as early as the 1850s, would not become commonplace until the twentieth century); and in the United States, everything from horseracing and cockfighting to beating and overloading working horses; cruelly handling, transporting, and slaughtering sheep and cattle; and force-feeding geese to make the delicacy pâté de foie gras. Unfortunately, the twenty-first-century ASPCA is still battling some of these issues.

Bergh then described the activities of the Royal Society for the Prevention of Cruelty to Animals in London, holding it up as a workable model for America. He concluded by assuring his audience that animal protection was not—as so many things were at the time—a complex political issue. "This is a matter purely of conscience; it has no perplexing side issues.... It is a moral question in all its aspects.... It is a solemn recognition of that greatest attribute of the Almighty Ruler of the universe, mercy."

Bergh's address was well received, and a committee was appointed on the spot to draft a charter for the new society. This was done swiftly, and Bergh traveled to Albany to pursue the matter in person. He later credited the help of his "very dear friend," State Senator Charles J. Folger, who later served as secretary of the treasury under President Chester Arthur, with getting the bill passed. Bergh also presented revisions to the state's anticruelty law, which had been on the books since 1830, but in Bergh's view was woefully inadequate. Within two months, the legislature approved the charter, and on April 10, 1866, the American Society for the Prevention of Cruelty to Animals officially was born. Nine days later, a new and much improved anticruelty bill became law. Reflecting Bergh's rationale for amending the existing statute, the new act was titled "For the More Effectual Prevention of Cruelty to Animals." Henry Bergh and the ASPCA were in business.

There are some ironies in the way the anticruelty law has changed since Bergh's day. The 1830 law and Bergh's revision both used the word "malicious" in describing the kind of act that would be considered criminal, even though it was recognized that proving malice in the treatment of an animal would be difficult at best. Some 130 years later, the ASPCA helped draft legislation in New York State that made it a felony to "intentionally" abuse or cause the death of an animal. It is every bit as difficult to prove intent as it was to prove malice, but now, as then, it is necessary to compromise in order to pass new legislation. The law in Bergh's day protected only farm animals by name, although "or other animal" made it possible to argue for cats, dogs, and other creatures. Today, in contrast, farm animals are excluded from the felony law. The penalty for conviction of cruelty to animals in 1866 was up to a year in the penitentiary or county jail, a fine of $250, or both. Today, nearly 150 years later, the penalty for a felony conviction is up to two years in jail and a fine of $5,000.

The speed with which Bergh accomplished his mission in Albany is nothing short of breathtaking by today's standards. Still, he was impatient. Every step of the process was described in the daily papers, and Bergh frequently chastised the state assembly for its unfathomable delay. It is impossible to overstate the role that journalists played in advancing or presumably in undermining an individual's or organization's agenda. In the society's first annual report, a class of membership called "corresponding members" was listed "to be chosen from among those who have aided the advancement of the society's objects, *including members of the press*" [emphasis added].

The city in the mid-nineteenth century boasted more than a dozen daily newspapers, of every political stripe, attesting to the interest of the populace in the minutiae of current events. And minutiae are what they got! The *New York Times* of May 22, 1866, published as complete a record of the society's first meeting, held the previous evening, as might be expected in the organization's own official minutes. It reported that a resolution was made to petition the city government to remove the slippery stone pavement on several main thoroughfares, as this so-called "Russ Pavement," named for Horace Russ, who installed it, was known to be particularly dangerous to horses. The *Times* duly reported:

This resolution gave rise to discussion of the best means to effect the object of the Society, and various ideas were ventilated, ending in the naming of a special committee to report upon the condition of the pavement of the city, and the best means to remedy the grievances complained of ... this committee to be empowered to communicate with experts, *through the Press* [emphasis added], so as to be enabled to place the matter, in all its bearings, before the Society.

Of course the intense scrutiny of a free press could and would work against a cause as well as for it, and during the twenty-two years that Bergh would lead the newly formed society, he would experience both amply.

The ASPCA was granted broad powers by the New York State legislature. Not only were members and agents of the society empowered to enforce the animal-cruelty laws, but the police force of New York City "as well as of all other places where police organizations exist" were required to aid the society in enforcing the law—not only as it existed then, but as it "may hereafter be enacted for the protection of dumb animals." The society wasted no time in making use of this provision of its charter. At its first meeting, William McMurray, treasurer of the Metropolitan Police, brought up the need to make sure that the police were aware of their new duty. August Belmont moved that Mayor Hoffman, who was also present, issue a bulletin that explained the society's duties and powers, and ask the police to assist in carrying out its mandate. The mayor, however, pointed out that it would be better for such a circular to come from police headquarters, since orders from the mayor's office "amounted to very little now-a-days," and this motion passed.

The following month, Police Superintendent John Kennedy, another founder, issued an order to the police captains. He explained that there was now a Society for the Prevention of Cruelty to Animals that was charged with the duty to enforce the anticruelty law, and that the new society had the right to require the assistance of the police. He instructed the captains to so inform their men and required their watchfulness and diligence in doing so. How convenient to have all the relevant parties at hand to resolve this first matter of business!

Nevertheless, all did not go smoothly, and Bergh often complained in the papers about the lack of cooperation he received from some members of the police force and of the city's magistrates, who were either uninformed about the new law or in some cases simply refused to hear any animal-cruelty cases. At the same time, Bergh never failed to publicly commend those officers, prosecutors, and judges who were helpful to the cause. For a number of years, the society's annual reports listed all of the cases that were tried, stating whether the defendant had been convicted or acquitted, what sentence had been handed down, and the name of the judge.

In some ways, the struggle of Bergh and his men in the nineteenth century is still the struggle of the ASPCA's humane law enforcement (HLE) officers today. When passed in 1866, the state's anticruelty statute was embedded in Agriculture and Markets Law. This was logical enough, as the only animals mentioned in the law were livestock and working equines. But the anticruelty statutes in New York State are still found in Agriculture and Markets. This means that many of New York City's 41,000 police officers are as unaware of the current law and of their duty in enforcing it as their counterparts were in 1866. The ASPCA has recently made huge strides in closing the knowledge gap in New York City. The fact that beginning in 2001, the society's HLE department has been featured in *Animal Precinct*, an hour-long reality show on the Animal Planet network, has raised awareness of New York's anticruelty law, of the work of the ASPCA's "animal cops," and of the collaboration between them and officers of the New York Police Department. In addition, the ASPCA for many years has bestowed a Humane Hero of the Year Award on those police officers and firefighters who have gone above and beyond the call of duty in rescuing animals. Whereas Bergh published the names of proanimal magistrates and praised particularly helpful police officers in his letters to the newspapers, New York City's finest and bravest today are celebrated each year at an annual gala event in a posh Manhattan hotel, to which the media is lured by the presence of live animal "heroes" as well. The tactics may be different, but the strategy is the same.

Bergh realized from the outset that he had to make the prevention of cruelty a passion and commitment of the public as well as of the society's members, who at that time were nominated and elected by current members. The society offered a "small reward" for tips about animals being mistreated. In his first annual report, Bergh published "Suggestions for the Guidance of Persons Desirous of Prosecuting Individuals Guilty of Cruelty to Animals." Three methods were described. The first was to give the offender into the custody of a police officer, whereupon the offender would be taken straight to court to appear before a magistrate. The second was to have a summons issued. For this, the citizen should make careful notes in writing of all the details that he or she witnessed, as well as the offender's name and address, and make a complaint to a magistrate. The third method was for a witness to appeal to the ASPCA to prosecute on his behalf, and it was suggested that this was the method to use in cases where the offender was thought likely to abscond or evade the summons. With months and years elapsing today between when an individual is charged and when his case is heard in New York City, it's hard to imagine a system of justice so swift and effective as this suggests.

It seems there is no one as audacious as an honest man with his eye on a worthy prize. Although Bergh persuaded the state legislature, in the matter of a few weeks, to approve a broad new law and give his society the power to enforce it, his audacity did not stop there. Within two years he was writing to the Honorable A. Oakey Hall, District Attorney for New York County—who of course was another of the society's founding patrons—asking him to make a motion in the state supreme court to have Bergh admitted to the bar, albeit without requiring him to pass any examination. Bergh argued that he needed this access "in behalf of the merciful cause to which I am devoting my life." Specifically, he needed it in order to prosecute cases outside New York City. Hall complied, and with the stroke of a pen, Bergh became an assistant district attorney. The next step was to gain permission to represent New York State in state court when jurisdiction lay there. Charles S. Fairchild, state attorney general, granted him that authority in 1876. Bergh clearly did not ask these favors for himself, but truly for the cause, and he made excellent use of them. He often spent whole days in court, trying as many as thirty or forty cases. He rarely lost. Bergh also asked to be made a member of the Police Commission and the Parks Commission, but in these attempts he failed.

On the very day that he returned triumphant from Albany, Bergh put his powers to the test. With a copy of the new anticruelty law and the ASPCA charter in his pocket, he strode forth to do good. Only one block from his home he saw a truckman beating his horse, a common enough sight in the city at that time. He ordered the man to stop, explaining that he was breaking the law. The man told him he was out of his mind. When he told the man to stop a second time, the fellow laughed at him and offered to debate the point with fists in the street. It was a sobering moment for Bergh. He realized that the citizens of New York were cut from a different cloth than the peasants in Russia, who were accustomed to obeying the orders of a gentleman.

Undaunted, Bergh tried again the next day. This time what he witnessed was a butcher's cart, bumping over the cobblestones with calves
on their way to slaughter. The animals were tied at the ankles and tossed
on top of one another in the wagon "like so much cordwood." Bergh
was successful in arresting the perpetrator, although he had to pursue the
cart for many blocks to do so. The man was taken before a magistrate,
fined ten dollars, and dismissed. The incident was fully described the next
day in an anonymous letter to the editor of the *New York Express*. There's
little doubt that the letter was written by Bergh himself. The day after
that, three men were arrested for similar offenses. Each received a ten-
dollar fine and a day in the city prison.

Bergh spent many hours every day in the streets, on the piers, around
the abattoirs, and in gaming halls, ever alert for animals being abused.
The majority of arrests and convictions were for cruelty to horses, both
by individuals who owned a single, overworked cart horse, or by omni-
bus companies and railway lines that pursued their profits at the expense
of the overloaded, lame, and exhausted animals who struggled to pull the
conveyances on rough and slippery pavement, up hills, in every weather.

Cows and other livestock also were much abused and made up a
substantial number of cases. One of the wretched practices of the day was
to save money on grain by feeding brewery swill to dairy cattle, which
not only sickened the animals over time but spoiled their milk, causing
illness in the children who drank it. The attention that "swill milk" cases
received in the press in the latter part of the nineteenth century presaged
the media frenzy that accompanied the first human deaths from "mad
cow" disease in the first years of the twenty-first. Was it the cruelty to
animals that caused the public outcry, or the threat to human health?
Bergh never discriminated among victims, setting a precedent for his
society to emulate. He was genuinely concerned about the quality of
meat in animals who were starved and stressed and tormented before
their deaths. This is likewise one argument in favor of humane treatment
of farm animals today.

From the outset, Bergh demonstrated that not some but all animals
were to be protected from cruelty, a stance that further supported his
contention that his cause was based on principle rather than sentiment.
He risked, and richly received, ridicule by bringing to court just weeks
into the ASPCA's life a case about chickens, charging that the fowl were
being plucked and boiled while still alive. Bergh had investigated the
matter and seen with his own eyes that this was true. The defense insisted
that the chickens were stabbed in the head beforehand, and that in any
case, a fowl was not an "animal" in the intent of the law, and moved for

dismissal. The court refused to entertain this notion. On cross examination, Bergh pointed out that decapitation, which would be swift and humane, wasn't being done because the chickens were sold by weight and the dealers were unwilling to forgo the additional income. Bergh lost the case. The judge ruled that since the animals had been stabbed in the brain before plucking, that willful or intentional cruelty had not been proven, and the defendants were acquitted.

An unfortunate side issue of the chicken case emerged in the papers and hurt Bergh both personally and in terms of public approval. It seems that on the same day his chicken case was being heard, the prison box contained a dozen men who were accused of wife beating, and the battered women were on hand as witnesses. The judge decided to take Bergh's case first, but the papers reported that Bergh had requested special consideration and the judge had granted it. Thus in the court of public opinion, Bergh was found guilty of caring more about abused chickens than about battered women.

If Bergh's "chicken case" made the press contemptuous, his "turtle case" made it vicious. In this instance, Bergh arrested the captain and crew of a vessel for the cruel manner in which they transported forty turtles from the tropics to New York. The crew had placed the turtles on their backs, pierced their fins, and threaded thongs through the holes to tie them together. The turtles were given no nourishment during the journey of several weeks. The argument advanced for the defense was that turtles were not animals—not that they were not animals in the intent of the law, but that they were not animals at all!

Bergh effectively countered that claim by reminding the court that there were only three kingdoms in nature: animal, mineral, and vegetable, and that since turtles surely were neither mineral nor vegetable, they must be animals. Unfortunately, the judge in the end decided that turtles were insects and unable to suffer. The captain and his crew were acquitted.

Although Bergh lost the case, he gained a great deal of publicity, as all of the papers covered the incredible case—doubtlessly the first of its kind in the world. Bergh was universally ridiculed for defending turtles. Caricaturists depicted him being embraced by a turtle. Years later, when he discussed this case, Bergh said it was the best thing that ever happened, because overnight everyone knew about the society and its objectives. Apparently he was an early believer in the adage that there's no such thing as bad publicity.

A significant aspect of the turtle case is that Bergh appealed to an outside expert on the subject of whether or not turtles feel pain when placed on their backs. He wrote to Dr. Louis Agassiz, a professor of comparative zoology at Harvard and the most prominent authority on biology in the country. Agassiz responded to Bergh in a thoughtful, respectful letter. He reasoned that because turtles placed on their backs for a long time will eventually die—and not because of lack of nourishment, since turtles were well known to be able to withstand long periods of time without nourishment—they must suffer from the unnatural position and pressure on their organs. Agassiz may have been the first "expert witness" in an animal-cruelty case. Today the testimony of ASPCA experts—from veterinarians and humane law enforcement officers to behaviorists—can help to win a conviction in prosecuting animal cruelty, or sometimes an acquittal in cases charging canine aggression.

Agassiz proved himself to be scrupulously objective. Subsequent to the turtle case, Bergh was doing battle with Phineas T. Barnum, of eventual Barnum & Bailey Circus fame. Bergh had many valid concerns about Barnum's treatment of animals. In this case, tipped off that Barnum was feeding live animals to his boa constrictors, Bergh charged the "ultimate showman" with cruelty to animals. Barnum, however, beat Bergh at his own game. He contacted Professor Louis Agassiz for his opinion on the matter, and Agassiz responded—incorrectly, as we've since learned—that snakes must be fed live prey. Bergh suffered humiliation in this case, and others, in which he tried to pin a cruelty charge on Barnum. In the end, however, Bergh was exonerated. Barnum, a native of Connecticut, retired there eventually, and apparently suffering a late-life change of heart, became a member of the ASPCA. He also founded the Bridgeport Society for the Prevention of Cruelty to Animals, and erected a monument to Henry Bergh in that city.

Another apparent late-life conversion accrued considerable benefit to the ASPCA. A French fur trapper named Louis Bonard was on his deathbed when he sent for Bergh. Bonard stated that he had long admired Bergh's work and wished to leave his property to the society. The ASPCA's charter clearly stated that it could not hold real estate. Bergh promptly turned the matter over to the society's first counsel, Hon. Elbridge T. Gerry, who spent two years on the case. Bonard's heirs contested the will, claiming that Bonard was insane, as no sane person would will his fortune for such a purpose. It came out during the lengthy trial that Bonard believed in reincarnation and feared he might return to Earth as a carriage horse. But the court ruled that Bonard's beliefs did not necessarily mean he was insane, and the will was upheld. Gerry was able to convince the New York State legislature—through the offices of none other than "Boss" Tweed—to amend the ASPCA's charter so as to allow it to hold real property. The Bonard estate was the society's first, and the funds it provided (less the considerable court costs) allowed the ASPCA to purchase a new headquarters building.

Sometimes Bergh was able to prevail on behalf of an animal without having to go to court at all. In one instance he was walking past a building under construction when he heard the faint sound of a cat meowing. Upon investigating, he found that the cat had crawled into a small space inside a wall, and rather than take the time or trouble to coax the cat out, the workmen had simply sealed the wall, imprisoning the cat inside. Bergh located the builder and insisted that the wall had to be taken down to remove the cat. It's hard to imagine how incredulous the builder must have been at such an order in 1866, especially considering the time, trouble, and expense that would be involved in complying with it. He protested long and loudly, but Bergh was unmoved, and in the end the wall was opened and the cat rescued.

One case that earned Bergh high marks from the press and the public was in breaking up the dogfighting ring of a particularly cruel and unwholesome character named Kit Burns. Burns was the impresario of the pit and ran a very active and profitable business in the basement of his saloon and gambling establishment called Sportsman's Hall. Every phase and aspect of the way he trained and conditioned his fighting dogs was cruel and uncaring. Fights were held several times a week before large crowds of men who bet money on which dog would win. Fights were either to the death or until one dog could no longer continue, at which time the losing dog would be tossed aside to die of his wounds. In point of fact, dogfighting is largely unchanged today, with the exception that Kit Burns was arrogant enough to advertise openly when a fight was to be held. He knew that Bergh and his agents would have to actually catch him in the act of goading a dog to fight in order to be convicted— the fact that dogs were fighting on his premises wasn't enough—and Burns was clever enough not to let that happen. But Bergh himself had the tenacity of a pit bull, and though it took several years, he eventually was able to get the evidence he needed. It involved carefully "casing the joint," recruiting enough police officers to block all entrances, the element of surprise, and the physicality of one police officer climbing up on the roof of Sportsman's Hall and dropping down through a skylight into the middle of the pit as the dogs were tearing one another apart while their owners urged them on. Of course the papers covered the arrest and arraignment of Burns and the thirty-some other "roughs" who were captured—the story made the front page of the *Times* on November 23, 1870—and all had the highest praise for Bergh's service in ridding the community of the blight that Burns and his bloody pit fights had been.

In 2007, the ASPCA again was praised for its role in investigating a dogfighting operation, this time involving the star quarterback of a professional football team. In addition to collecting forensic evidence in the case, the ASPCA was tapped to lead the behavioral evaluation of the dogs seized by authorities and to make recommendations to the U.S. Department of Agriculture and the federal prosecutor on the disposition of the dogs.

Bergh did not discriminate in his pursuit of justice for animals who were used in bloody "entertainment." He wrote and spoke out about the cruelties of horseracing, foxhunting, "coursing" hare with dogs, and using live pigeons for what amounted to target practice—even inventing the alternative of a "gyropigeon," which simulated a bird in flight. These "sporting" activities were recreational pastimes of wealthier people, including some of Bergh's personal friends and at least one of the ASPCA's founding patrons.

Preventing cruelty was Bergh's primary concern, but he recognized that cruelty had two sources: those who knew better, and those who didn't. From the outset, Bergh was inclined to educate and warn individuals whom he sensed were not wantonly cruel but were simply uninformed and uneducated about the law and the impact of their actions. Twenty-first century ASPCA HLE officers do the same. Viewers of *Animal Precinct* have seen agents "work with" rather than arrest pet owners whose animals are suffering from neglect, if they determine that the individuals care about their pets but simply don't know how to care for them properly or may not have realized their responsibility in providing regular grooming, appropriate food, water, and shelter, as well as veterinary care.

Although Henry Bergh had chosen the prevention of cruelty to lower animals as his life's work, he was passionate about protection for other victims who were voiceless. By 1870, his actions on behalf of animals were well known, and he began to attract the attention of people concerned about the treatment of another species of abused creation: children.

In June 1871 Bergh was approached by a woman who was greatly concerned about the welfare of a young girl who lived near her. The woman had observed Mary Ann Larkin beating Emily Thompson for up to an hour at a time. Bergh decided to send some of his agents to evaluate the situation. When they confirmed that little Emily had certainly been beaten and bore vivid black and blue bruises, Bergh huddled with his attorney, Elbridge Gerry. There were some laws that protected children from excessive beating and physical mistreatment. However, there were no real legal strategies available to remove a child from an abusive home. For all intents and purposes, children were chattel. They belonged to their parents or to other adults where they lived.

Gerry, however, came up with an ingenious application of the writ of habeas corpus that he believed would allow authorities to seize a child in danger of further mistreatment. Working under Gerry's guidance, Bergh's men removed Emily from Larkin's home, and charges were brought against Larkin. During the trial, Larkin claimed that both of Emily Thompson's parents had died, and she was entrusted with the young girl's care. Larkin's neighbor testified in court that she had seen Emily beaten. Other neighbors corroborated this. However, when Emily Thompson was brought forward, she denied that she had been beaten, even though she still bore the evidence of her mistreatment. Apparently, she was loath to implicate the only woman she had known as a mother. The judge found Larkin guilty, but suspended the sentence and, given the lack of another option for placement, returned Emily to Larkin's custody.

Bergh was appalled that while the legal strategy had apparently succeeded, the outcome left Emily in an abusive home. In a final twist, Violet Bickom from New Jersey had read about the case in the newspapers, and ferried across the Hudson to track down Henry Bergh. Bickom was Emily Thompson's grandmother, whom Larkin had also claimed was dead. Emily returned to New Jersey with her grandmother.

In 1873 Bergh was again contacted by someone concerned about the welfare of a child. Etta Angell Wheeler was a social worker in the Hell's Kitchen neighborhood of New York City. An elderly woman whom she cared for implored that she do something to aid a young girl in the apartment across the hall from her. She rarely if ever saw the child since it seemed that she was constantly confined in the apartment, but she could readily hear the girl cry out, and awful sounds of her being beaten.

When Wheeler investigated, she was shocked by what she discovered. Little Mary Ellen was poorly dressed in the drafty, cold apartment, and clearly bruised. Wheeler approached the police and other authorities but they all demurred, unwilling to challenge the time-honored premise that a parent has total license in the treatment of her children. It was Wheeler's niece who suggested that she contact Henry Bergh. His reputation for kindness must surely extend to children as well.

Wheeler went to Bergh's office and presented her concerns to him. After the Emily Thompson case, Bergh was cautious, and asked if she would provide her story in writing for him and allow him some time to consider it. Wheeler responded with such a compelling statement that Bergh sent it on to Gerry, asking for advice once again. In the meantime, Bergh sent one of his agents, in the guise of a census worker, to confirm

Wheeler's observations. When the agent came back and described what he had seen, Bergh and Gerry again moved into action.

Gerry secured a warrant under the writ of habeas corpus, and Bergh's men enlisted the aid of New York City police to remove Mary Ellen from the apartment. Bergh arranged to have Mary Ellen brought directly to the court, and ensured that newspapermen were notified. This time, Bergh would employ his public relations skills along with Gerry's legal brilliance. Hardened reporters and authorities alike were aghast when Mary Ellen made her appearance. The waif was wearing a threadbare cotton dress, and had been wrapped in a horse blanket to protect her from the cold during the carriage ride downtown. Her black and blue marks had been augmented by an ugly cut on her face, the result of an angry blow with a pair of scissors by her foster mother, Mary Connolly. Two indictments were brought against Connolly. She was found guilty of assault and battery, and sentenced to a year of confinement and hard labor. At first Mary Ellen was made a ward of the court, but Wheeler and Bergh objected that she would not receive the care she needed in an institution. Eventually Mary Ellen was placed with Wheeler's sister, who lived in upstate New York. In a remarkable show of resilience, she grew into a happy young woman who married and was a loving mother.

Unlike the Emily Thompson case, which left little impact, the Mary Ellen case drew extensive publicity. Among the many reporters who covered the story was a recent immigrant from Denmark, Jacob Riis. Riis was just starting what would be a legendary career as a muckraking journalist and social reformer. Riis and the other reporters soon made the Mary Ellen case well known throughout the city. They used the story to demand change in the way that children were treated. Songs about Mary Ellen were written, and her story became a standard part of the curriculum for social workers.

Unfortunately, in their eagerness to tell the heart-wrenching tale, Riis and the others created a myth that has only recently been corrected. They suggested that there had been no laws to protect children, and that Bergh claimed that if nothing else, Mary Ellen would be given the same protection as a dog in the street, and used the powers of the ASPCA and the anticruelty law to exact justice for Mary Ellen. The truth, in fact, was that Bergh made every effort to ensure that his actions in this case were not seen as part of his official duties as president of the ASPCA. Moreover, to ensure that the protection of children was viewed as clear and separate from protecting animals, Bergh, Elbridge Gerry, and a wealthy gentleman named James D. Wright, formed the Society for the Prevention of Cruelty to Children (SPCC). Many humane groups around the country, having already copied Bergh in the formation of their animal-protection societies, also copied his actions in protection of children. Unlike Bergh, however, they often combined the functions of animal and child protection in one organization. Bergh would frequently voice his opposition to this arrangement, arguing that when combined, neither cause would garner the support or attention it demanded.

Henry Bergh's health had begun to decline in the early part of the 1880s. His collarbone was broken in a street accident in 1883. His wife, Matilda, had been an invalid for a number of years, dying in May 1887, depriving him of a valued source of support. The many years of braving the elements to protect animals in the city had taken a toll on his health. Bergh had begun his crusade for animals at the age of 53. More than twenty years later, he still stalked the streets of New York on the lookout for animals who needed his protection.

Bergh was ill and confined to bed on March 11, 1888. The weather was warm and trees were beginning to bud. Later in the day it began to rain. Overnight, the rain turned to snow, and winds up to 50 mph. churned the snow into the Blizzard of Eighty-Eight, which paralyzed New York City and the entire Northeast for days. When the great storm began, it became clear that Bergh's condition was declining. His nephew sent for the doctor, but the snow delayed his travel, and he arrived just fifteen minutes before Henry Bergh died on the morning of March 12, 1888.

Bergh's funeral was at St. Mark's Episcopal Church on March 16. Numerous dignitaries attended to honor the man who changed the way we care for animals. Legend has it that a young girl arrived at the door with a small dog, and the rector allowed her to enter in homage to Bergh's great lifework. Burial at Green-Wood Cemetery in Brooklyn was delayed until March 24, in the aftermath of the storm. Bergh's old nemesis, P. T. Barnum, was one of his pallbearers.

Chapter 3

One Hundred Years of Animal Control

When the ASPCA agreed to take over the city pound in 1894, it was the first time that an SPCA or humane group was officially designated to fulfill the "animal control" needs for the city. On March 8, 1894, the governor of New York State signed a bill that authorized the ASPCA to perform the following tasks:

1. Issue dog licenses and renewals;
2. Supply tags, notify owners of renewals, return lost dogs to owners, pay for inspector and clerical salaries;
3. Seize unlicensed dogs and any cats without identification;
4. Maintain shelters for lost, stray, or homeless animals;
5. Provide a painless death for unclaimed animals or animals not placed with new owners.

Shortly thereafter the society acquired a $100' \times 25'$ building to serve as an animal shelter. Within the first eight months, the ASPCA handled 22,028 dogs, cats, and other animals. Of these, 632 were returned to their owners. This work was accomplished with the aid of twenty-two staff members, and eight horses who were used to pull four ambulances and two wagons. The staff members were full-time employees and were paid a wage for their labors. Unlike the previous dogcatchers for the city pound, their income did not depend on the number of animals they caught or who were reclaimed by owners. The ASPCA was generally praised for its work in these early days. People were happy that their dogs were no longer subject to abduction from their yards by the dogcatcher, and the strays who were a problem were being managed more effectively. Seeing a good thing, officials in Brooklyn, still a separate city, approached

31

the ASPCA to run its pound as well, and in 1896, ASPCA shelter services expanded to cover Brooklyn. Even as the society embarked upon this grand experiment, then-president John P. Haines expressed reservations about the costs that the society would absorb and whether the license fees it was authorized to collect would be adequate to fully support the operations.

The animal shelter of this era was simple in design and construction. It resembled a stable in many ways, with several large open pens with straw bedding typically used for holding dogs, and some cages for cats and other small animals who might come in. There were separate pens for nursing mothers and females in heat. People looking for a lost dog, or wishing to acquire a new dog, were allowed to look in the pens and point at the dog they thought was theirs, or the one they wanted. When a pen was filled, dogs were removed and euthanized to make room for the new dogs who would come in later that day, the next day, and the day after.

In 1889, the city pounds had introduced chloroform chambers for euthanizing unwanted animals. The ASPCA used these chambers in the beginning, but work to develop more effective and efficient systems for euthanasia continued. Eventually, steel chambers that used illuminating gas were employed. Illuminating gas, derived from liquefied coal, was piped throughout the city to provide fuel for lighting. It was readily available and effectively asphyxiated animals.

Over the ensuing century, the animal-control operation would become the society's central focus. It would account for the majority of its employees and most of its budget. It would also consume the major attention of the management staff and board, and would come to define the society in the mind of the public. In a prescient and cogent statement that remains relevant to this day, Haines articulated the ASPCA's three-fold mission:

1. As a local society in the City of New York, exercising peculiar functions, which have been committed to no other similar society elsewhere;
2. As a state society empowered to intervene anywhere in New York State;
3. As the ASPCA, bound by its traditions, charter, and bylaws to care for the cause of animal protection everywhere in the United States.

Over the next several decades, Haines and the ASPCA would see hundreds of other SPCAs and humane groups follow their lead and take up the animal control duties for their communities as well.

The need to protect working horses from cruel treatment was the driving force in the origin and development of the ASPCA and other SPCAs, but by 1900 the number of ambulance calls for horses was in decline.

With the introduction of electric trolleys, fewer horses were used for the hard work of hauling the often overloaded railcars. SPCAs began to expend more and more of their resources on running shelters for dogs and cats. Some observers of the humane movement believe that this change in focus served to blunt the movement's impact for much of a century. Constant financial woes due to the costs of running the municipal shelters forced humane groups to reduce their attention to vivisection, animals raised for food, and the treatment of wildlife.

Despite financial concerns, the ASPCA's shelter and license operations grew dramatically. The society was operating shelters in all five New York City boroughs. In 1911, the society moved its Manhattan operations to Twenty-fourth Street and Avenue A. Hundreds of staff members cleaned kennels, drove rescue vehicles, and worked as clerks. Each of the shelters largely operated as an independent entity. The shelter director was responsible for all operations within his facility, coordinating staff schedules and operations. Each shelter had its own motor pool, with mechanics to service the ambulances and other vehicles that were being used. The motor pool was a beehive of activity. In the year 1927 the society operated a fleet of forty-seven cars and ambulances that logged 880,000 miles in New York City. In addition to catching free-roaming strays and collecting injured animals from the streets, the ASPCA responded to over 140,000 requests for home pickups, resulting in more than 200,000 animals received.

The Great Depression devastated the world and American economies, and pets suffered along with their owners. Thousands of people, barely able to feed themselves, turned their dogs and cats in to ASPCA shelters, preferring to see them die a painless death rather than starve. Many owners could not afford to buy a dog license, and this reduced revenue to the society for shelter operations. The charitable contributions that funded humane law enforcement and education, and offset shelter deficits, also declined. The society lost many members due to financial hardship.

In the 1920s and early 1930s, just before and during the years of the Great Depression, the society handled nearly 300,000 animals per year. Thousands of these were reclaimed by owners, and thousands more were placed in new homes. The sad reality, however, was that the vast majority of the animals entering the shelters were euthanized. For example, more than 280,000 dogs, cats, and other animals were euthanized in 1928. Most of these were cats, accounting for 216,000 animals. At this point in time, the public was not asking how many animals were dying in the ASPCA shelters, or in other shelters around the country. This question would wait until the years following World War II.

In addition to regular maintenance on vehicles and facilities, the ASPCA did build and open a new shelter in Queens in 1934. Consistent with established pattern, the construction of the new facility was funded by the ASPCA through charitable contributions. Even though it would be used to support the animal-control program for the city, no public funds were ever provided for construction or capital improvement. The names of individuals who contributed $500 or more to this campaign for the shelter in Queens were inscribed on a plaque.

The war years were a struggle for the ASPCA, as they were for the nation in general. Steel was scarce, as it was needed to produce war materiel. Dog license tags were not a high priority, and the society switched to pressed fiberboard tags during the war. Gas was rationed, and vehicle use was limited. Broken-down ambulances and cars sat in the shelter motor pools waiting for parts. Meat was rationed, and Dr. Mark Morris, founder of the Hills pet-food line, scrambled to come up with alternative diets for America's pets. The ASPCA worked with the Civil Defense authorities to provide first-aid training for pets who might be injured during the enemy bombing raids that everyone feared.

Not to be overlooked were the numbers of ASPCA staff who were called to serve in the military during the war. The roll call went across the organization: clerks, animal care staff, ambulance drivers. Various materials from the society, including newsletters to members and staff, listed the names of those going off to war and those returning. Dr. Norman Johnson, one of the staff veterinarians, was among several who served during the war by providing care for horses, still used in some units. Dr. Johnson returned to the ASPCA after the war and retired in 1990 after fifty years of service. Others were not so fortunate. Especially poignant were notices in society publications of those who had been killed.

In 1944 the ASPCA survived a confrontation with the City of New York over services and funding, a scenario that would recur several times in the next half-century. A rabies epidemic had struck among the dogs in New York. The mayor and city health officials wanted to require the ASPCA to hold all dogs suspected of being rabid for six months. The society balked at this order, claiming that holding dogs for this length of time was not justified, and that the added cost would overwhelm the society's budget and its ability to conduct other needed shelter operations. Dog license fees had not been increased since the original bill in 1894: two dollars for a new license and one dollar for a renewal.

When Mayor Fiorello LaGuardia learned of the society's position, he was enraged, and arranged to have a bill introduced in the state legislature to strip the ASPCA of its authority to issue dog licenses and collect the fees. Those powers would be transferred to the city. The ASPCA opposed the bill, as did most people in New York who cared about animals. New York radio personality Pegeen Fitzgerald lobbied against the bill during the popular daytime WOR radio show she cohosted with her husband. The bill was defeated, but fifty years after the city prevailed in its courtship of the ASPCA, the ardor had begun to cool. It would be another fifty years, many of them rocky, before the relationship would be dissolved.

The first years after the war were filled with some optimism for Americans. Worldwide fascism had been defeated. The United States was clearly established as a dominant world power. The Korean War and the Cold War, with its ever-looming scenario of world annihilation, were still to come. But in the mid-1940s, the men were home, and factories turned their efforts from tanks and planes to cars, sewing machines, and consumer goods that had been in short supply during the war years. The 1948 ASPCA annual meeting attracted more than 600 people to the Ritz-Carlton in Manhattan, and included a screening of the 1941 MGM short film about Bergh's life, *The Great Meddler*. New ASPCA president, John D. Beals, Jr., talked about other postwar eras and how they stimulated the formation of new animal protection societies.

The good times for the ASPCA were quickly swept away when it was struck by a delayed bombshell left over from the war. Among the men returning from overseas were many wounded veterans. The hospital system for veterans needed to expand to meet the need. On November 29, 1948, the Monday after Thanksgiving, the ASPCA was notified that its Manhattan shelter and hospital at Twenty-fourth Street and Avenue A was being condemned under eminent domain to make way for a new veterans' hospital. The society would have until April 1, 1950, to vacate the location. The federal government offered just $304,000 in compensation for the property.

The society had some property available on the Upper East Side of New York at the corner of Ninety-second Street and York Avenue. However, architects and engineers hired by the ASPCA estimated that it would cost at least $950,000 to build a new facility at that location. The society immediately embarked on a multifaceted effort to design, build, and fund the new building. Every effort would be made to construct a modern facility that made the best use of new ideas and materials to serve the needs of the society and New York's animals.

Fundraising events were held in the city, and an appeal was announced in the newspapers. Donors large and small were sought. A "Brick for a

Buck" campaign was rolled out to help build the new ASPCA. Additional funds were raised when the ASPCA board decided to sell its headquarters building at 50 Madison Avenue and consolidate the executive offices at the new shelter and hospital. They also appealed the condemnation award from the government, and sought extra time to design, build, and move to the new location. It was just over two years from notice to completion. On December 9, 1950, the ASPCA occupied its new headquarters, hospital, and shelter at 441 East Ninety-second Street. Among the many features of the new facility was a set of dog runs on the roof to allow hospital patients fresh air and exercise. Heating coils ran through the roof to melt snow, allowing the runs to be used year-round. A huge art deco sculpture hung on the side of the building entitled "Humanity of Man Before a Group of Ageless Animals," a gift to the ASPCA for its new building by sculptors Wilhelm Hunt Diedrich and John Terken. The new building, with its striking sculpture, was within sight of the FDR Drive, the major north-south artery on Manhattan's East Side, and it became a familiar landmark for two generations of New Yorkers before the society sold the location in 1992 and moved halfway down the block. Too large and heavy to be hung on the society's new building, the sculpture was put in storage until April 2006, when it was placed at the foot of Henry Bergh's mausoleum in Green-Wood Cemetery as part of the society's 140th anniversary celebration.

The post–World War II era, much like the decades following the Civil War, was a time of significant social upheaval and change. Reform was in the air after the Civil War. The abolition of slavery was accompanied by greater roles for women and greater attention to the treatment of children and workers. The era also spawned the birth of the ASPCA and the American animal protection movement. The years after World War II gave rise to renewed efforts in many of these same areas. The war effort required an unprecedented number of women to work outside the home, many in nontraditional roles. The fictional character "Rosie the Riveter," a cultural icon of the war years, represented the millions of American women who worked in factories and shipyards. Once the men returned from military service, many of these women were unwilling to fade back into their former restrictive roles in the home. At the same time, the GI Bill afforded a generation of veterans the opportunity to attend college and buy homes, helping to create the modern American middle class of professionals. Automobiles and trucks now dominated the transportation arteries, and the occasional horse-drawn fruit and vegetable cart in the city was a quaint novelty. By the 1960s, the Civil Rights Movement and then efforts to end the Vietnam War brought a new look and vigor to social activism. (The ASPCA played a role here, too, when its agents arrested peace activists who released pigeons into Grand Central Station in 1968, and investigated the release of twenty-five white mice in City Hall in 1974 by the Gay Activists Alliance to protest the defeat of a homosexual-rights bill.) Many old institutions and practices were challenged. They would either need to change or be swept away.

The ASPCA was one of the old institutions that found itself challenged. Throughout the next several decades, ASPCA publications would note contradictory impressions of the society: on January 21, 1968, the *Daily News* included the organization in an editorial about organizations that made America great. A short time later, a group of activists picketed outside the society's headquarters to protest its policies and practices.

The year 1951 brought some good news when the state legislature voted to raise the dog license fee from two dollars to three dollars. It was hoped that this increase would ease the strain on the budget for the operation of the licensing, animal rescue, and shelter services. However, this event was quickly followed by another challenge.

During World War II, biomedical science made valuable contributions to the prevention of disease among soldiers and the treatment of battlefield injuries. The promise of still greater contributions was palpable, but would depend on the availability of needed resources. One of those resources was animals who could be used as experimental subjects. Scientists turned to the nation's animal shelters, where millions of unwanted dogs and cats were being killed every year. Why not use these unwanted animals as subjects? Why buy research subjects when the local pound could provide them for free?

Many animal shelters, including the ASPCA, balked at this prospect. Bergh and other founders of the American humane movement had been passionate antivivisectionists. As far back as 1889, impounded dogs were being sought for medical research, and Judge Gideon J. Tucker, who had drafted Bergh's original anticruelty statute in 1866, wrote to then-Mayor Hugh L. Grant to "respectfully protest against the proposition made to you to hand over living stray dogs from the pound for anatomical purposes." But in 1951, the research establishment prevailed upon state and local governments to pass laws that would require shelters to provide animals for research. This practice, known as "pound seizure," reawakened old and deeply held feelings about the use of animals in research. The ASPCA was thrust into the middle of the debate in New York State. In his time, Bergh had tried repeatedly to have the practice of vivisection outlawed in the state, only to be rebuffed each time by the legislature. Consequently, when the Metcalf-Hatch pound-seizure bill was introduced in Albany in 1951, the ASPCA was expected to voice vigorous objections. Many in the humane movement were stunned when the ASPCA failed to mount a strong effort to block the bill, and the ASPCA earned the enmity of many animal activists for years to come.

The ASPCA board and management were fully aware of the controversy that they were courting. However, they were engaged in a delicate political calculus. The pound-seizure bill had overwhelming support in the state legislature. It was obvious to the board that the bill was going to become law regardless of its opposition. It would have been simple enough for them to oppose the bill, fret and fume about its potential harm to animals, and then deal with its requirements when it became law. This approach would at least have kept other humane groups from condemning the ASPCA. The board chose a different course. It would not oppose the legislation, but would extract a concession: ASPCA agents would be permitted to inspect all laboratories in the state that used animals in research, whether or not they received those animals from the ASPCA.

Metcalf-Hatch became law in New York State on July 1, 1952, and before the end of the year, the ASPCA had launched a laboratory-inspection program. So it was that in the years following the passage of the pound-seizure law, ASPCA annual reports dutifully reported the number of dogs and cats that had been requisitioned for use in research laboratories. The reports also indicated the number of inspections performed. These inspections predated any federal requirements for oversight for laboratory animals. The society went still further. ASPCA veterinarians developed training courses for laboratory technicians and veterinarians in the proper care and husbandry of research animals. By 1968, a special class in Spanish for laboratory technicians had been added.

In 1972, public criticism and changes in the biomedical industry moved the ASPCA to call for the repeal of pound seizure. The ASPCA also refused to comply with the requirements of Metcalf-Hatch, and no longer supplied animals for experimentation. This became part of the ASPCA legislative agenda in Albany until 1979, when state lawmakers voted to repeal the law. Despite this victory, and the ASPCA's leadership role in lobbying for the change, stories persisted into the 1990s that the ASPCA continued to supply shelter animals for scientific research.

The booming media market in the 1960s and 1970s provided the ASPCA with a profile in the public eye that it had not enjoyed since the days of Henry Bergh. Network television and major publications ranging from *Glamour, Family Circle,* and *Good Housekeeping* did feature stories on the ASPCA and its programs. Several producers approached the society to develop a regular television series about the ASPCA. A couple of these filmed pilot episodes. No such series ever graced the television screen until 2001, when Anglia Television, Ltd., an English production company, developed *Animal Precinct*, a reality show that featured the ASPCA's humane law enforcement officers as they went on daily patrol to investigate complaints of cruelty to animals in New York City. The series attracted millions of viewers and brought the ASPCA and the issue of animal cruelty to the attention of animal lovers across the nation and around the world.

Based on membership lists in the society's annual reports, women had outnumbered men as supporters of the organization almost from the beginning. Nevertheless, the ASPCA board of directors was an all-male group for more than one hundred years. That changed in December 1971 when Gretchen Wyler was elected to the board. Wyler was a well-known Broadway star and a passionate animal activist. Her landmark election received major media attention, and Wyler soon became an active public voice on behalf of animals. She frequently appeared on radio, television, and in print to talk about ASPCA programs and services and the importance of proper pet care. In June 1972, Wyler was heard in radio spots countering the "children before dogs" campaign led by Fran Lee, a television personality and consumer advocate in the 1960s and 1970s, that questioned providing care and treatment for animals while there were children in need. This campaign was reminiscent of a 1969 book by Kathleen Szasz—*Petishism: Pets and Their People in the Western World*—which questioned the mounting obsession that Americans had with pets and its impact on society. Wyler pointed out that kindness to children and kindness to pets were not mutually exclusive.

By the late 1960s and early 1970s, greater attention was being paid to the number of animals being killed in animal shelters. It was no longer enough for a shelter to provide humane housing and a humane death. The demand now was that something be done about the horrific numbers—estimated to be in the tens of millions—of "excess" dogs and cats who were killed each year in the United States. Surgical sterilization of dogs and cats had been practiced for decades. More often than not, it was performed as a matter of convenience for pet owners. Male cats were castrated to prevent urine spraying, fighting, and roaming. Female dogs were spayed to eliminate bleeding and discharge during heat. Now the procedures would be employed in a massive campaign to prevent the reproduction of dogs and cats, in the hope of stemming the tide of unwanted pets that were flooding animal shelters. The campaign would become a cornerstone of the ASPCA's program, and that of animal sheltering groups across the country, for the next forty years.

What today seems to be an obvious decision was subject to extended discussion at meetings of the ASPCA board. In 1972, the board voted to require that anyone who adopted a pet from one of the ASPCA shelters agree to have the pet sterilized. There was concern that people would be less willing to adopt a pet with this stipulation, but the board decided that in the long run, it would be better to adopt out fewer pets, if sterilization resulted in smaller numbers of unwanted pets being born.

Media coverage was massive when the new policy went into effect in 1973. People adopting a pet were required to sign a "contract" agreeing to have the dog or cat sterilized within six months of adoption. The ASPCA hospital would perform the surgery for free, or adopters could choose to take the pet to a veterinarian of their choice. While it was unlikely that the society would be able to track down every adopter to ensure that she fulfilled her commitment, the new policy was as important for its educational value as it was for its practical impact. Encil Rains, executive vice president at the time, appeared on all local television affiliates and in all New York newspapers, as the Associated Press and United Press International news wire services covered the change in policy. Gretchen Wyler's appearance on the *Mike Douglas Show* brought the issue to a national audience.

Those who feared that adoptions would go down were proved correct, as fewer pets were adopted in 1973 than in 1972. However, the long-term effect that the board had hoped for was achieved. Over the next two decades, the number of animals entering the ASPCA shelters showed a steady decline.

Some of the adoption policies from this era stand in stark contrast to popular thinking about adoptions today. No fee was charged for an adopted animal, and pets were readily promoted as wonderful presents for loved ones. In fact, in the weeks leading up to Christmas, ASPCA press releases encouraged giving a puppy or kitten, dog or cat as a gift. If you made your choice early, the shelter would hold the pet until December 24 so you could surprise your children on Christmas Day. Attitudes about giving pets as gifts changed greatly over the years, and the practice is now generally discouraged. However, research shows that pets received as gifts have no increased risk of relinquishment.

The ASPCA adoption campaign near Halloween had an interesting twist. ASPCA staff made a point of exploiting the black cat–Halloween connection as a way to debunk negative myths about black cats and to promote adoptions. Barbara Miller, head of the Education department at the time, dressed as a witch, and with several black kittens in tow, appeared on the *Romper Room* television show for children, to impress upon kids that black cats didn't bring bad luck and would make great pets. Elsewhere around the country, many shelters still refuse to adopt out black cats during the Halloween season, fearing that people will simply use them as props for Halloween parties or mistreat them in some way. They do this despite the lack of evidence to support such policies.

Wyler did not rest at being a voice for animals and the ASPCA. She was instrumental in organizing the society's first volunteer program, and took an active interest in the animal shelters. This interest eventually put her at odds with her fellow board members, and in January 1975 led her and another member of the board, Linda Meyer, to sue the ASPCA. The suit was settled in July 1976. The results of the lawsuit brought an end to an era in the organization's life and started it on a path toward modernization in philosophy and practice. In retrospect, the Wyler-Meyer lawsuit goaded the ASPCA to make changes that would have been needed one way or the other in the years to come. While it did result in some ill will, it also created an environment where change was expected. The ASPCA made many changes in the next two decades. Most significantly, in 1992, the board voted to no longer perform animal-control duties for the City of New York. In his time, Henry Bergh hadn't trusted the city. One hundred years later, his society decided he was right.

In the 1970s, a key criticism of the ASPCA was its use of "decompression chambers" to euthanize shelter animals. Introduced in the years after World War II, high-altitude or "decompression" chambers kill animals by suffocation when air is rapidly removed from a sealed container. The American Veterinary Medical Association approved the practice, but it had limited support among animal advocates and the public, who wanted shelters to adopt euthanasia by intravenous injection of sodium pentobarbital as standard practice. Arguments advanced in favor of retaining the decompression chamber were both the expense and the level of staff training required to euthanize by injection, as well as the negative impact on staff morale of having direct contact with thousands of animals each week as they died. In May 1976, animal shelter groups throughout the state of New York gathered in Erie County to develop plans to oppose the abolition of decompression chambers in New York State.

Funding issues were a constant concern for the society in this era. The sale of dog licenses no longer provided enough money to support the shelter system. The city's growing population and increased demand for services placed an unmanageable burden on the society. In December 1970, the ASPCA closed three suburban animal shelters that it was operating. Service fees introduced at the city shelters were protested. In 1973, Helen Jones, president of the Society for Animal Rights, and City

Council member Carter Burden, served the ASPCA with a lawsuit challenging the legality of the service charges. The fees were not rescinded, but public support waxed and waned.

Oftentimes the society was caught in the middle of changing attitudes and expectations regarding animals. For example, conflicts erupted when part of a community called for greater diligence in having strays picked up, but another part objected to having those animals go to the ASPCA shelter where they were likely to be euthanized. At the heart of the conundrum was the fact that there simply was no other group able to pick up the animals but not euthanize them.

In 1974, Councilman Burden proposed the creation of a city Department of Animal Affairs. While the ASPCA opposed the concept because it believed the city lacked the experienced staff and physical facilities necessary to do the job, there was no groundswell of support for the idea at the time. What was clear was that a great many people were not happy with the ASPCA's performance, but no one had a better idea. No other group seemed ready to commit the staff and resources needed to provide services for the entire City of New York. One obvious path to improved services—more funding—was blocked by the financial woes of New York City. In 1977, even as the ASPCA negotiated with the city for additional funding, employee unions at the society threatened to strike if any staff were laid off or terminated as a result of shelter closings or phaseouts. In September of that year, the City of New York agreed to provide an additional $103,000 per month to help keep all five full-service shelters open.

One of the enduring results of the Wyler-Meyer lawsuit was the addition of John F. Kullberg, Ed.D., to the board of directors. Kullberg was a protégé of Christine Stevens, the socially prominent founder of the Animal Welfare Institute (AWI) in Washington, D.C. in 1951. AWI spearheaded the passage of the Animal Welfare Act of 1966, the first federal legislation to set minimum standards of care for animals used in research, exhibition, and commerce. Continued issues with management performance at the ASPCA led the board to appoint Kullberg as acting executive director in January 1978. An educator with a strong background in ethics and legislative activism, he took over a troubled organization in turbulent times.

Kullberg's "acting" title was soon removed, and he began an aggressive effort to upgrade ASPCA shelter programs and reestablish the ASPCA's role as a national organization. One of the first challenges he took on in 1978 was to convert euthanasia methods from decompression to lethal injection of sodium pentobarbital.

In this era before every neighborhood had a private veterinary hospital and before pet owners were in the habit of obtaining routine care for their dogs and cats, it was the animal shelter where "humane services" such as euthanasia were performed, and the ASPCA's shelter veterinarians were already euthanizing animals by injection upon the request of pet owners who were willing to pay an extra $25 for the service. Nevertheless, many staff believed that conversion to the injection method for all animals would be impossible, given the additional cost and the need to safeguard the drug from abuse. Several staff were assigned to research the procedure, including procurement of the drug, costs, legal requirements, and development of an implementation process.

ASPCA veterinarians were deployed to train shelter staff to hold animals during euthanasia. The society was operating five shelters, seven days a week, twenty-four hours a day at that time. This complicated the conversion process since new work schedules were required to ensure that a veterinarian and an assisstant to hold the animal were available at night and on weekends. In the end, shelter veterinarians accepted responsibility for performing euthanasia and maintaining the records required with the use of a controlled substance. While the change demanded a substantial effort across the organization, the actual process of converting to injection euthanasia may have been less traumatic than the concern about making the change.

During the 1980s the society continued to deal with financial problems, the demand for services, and criticism of those services. Financial audits of the society forecast bankruptcy by the mid-1980s unless drastic action was taken to reduce the losses incurred by running shelter services for the City of New York. Repeated calls by the ASPCA to allow for inflationary increases in the dog license fees were rebuffed by both the city and the state. No politician wants to be blamed for raising taxes, and New York politicians certainly had no interest in raising taxes when they could not control where and how the money was spent. To avoid a complete financial collapse, the ASPCA closed its shelters in Queens, Staten Island, and the Bronx.

Officials in the three affected boroughs were understandably upset. However, instead of working to find the money to maintain a full shelter program, they banded together to revise the 1894 state law that originally gave the society the authority to issue dog licenses and operate shelters for the City of New York. They believed that closing the shelters was a ploy on the part of the ASPCA to extract additional funding from the city. They did not accept or understand the true cost of running the shelter system, and believed that the society was adequately funded to maintain the program. The state legislature voted to amend the 1894 law, allowing the city to give the ASPCA eighteen months' notice if it decided that it no longer wanted the ASPCA to carry out its animal control services. In a spirit of "fairness," the amendment also allowed the ASPCA to give the city eighteen months' notice if it decided it would no longer collect dog-license fees for the city or provide city-requested shelter services.

By 1988, even with the closure of three shelters, the ASPCA was running an annual deficit of $2 million on the city animal-control program. The cost to the society went well beyond money, however. Closing three shelters and reducing the number of rescue ambulances drained public confidence and support for the organization. A vicious spiral ensued as cuts in service further reduced support for the organization, resulting in even less funding for an already crippled program. Coupling these public relations problems with a never-ending game of "chicken" with city officials could have only one result: an organization on the edge of crisis.

With no relief in sight, the society took unexpected advantage of the amendment to the 1894 dog license law. On October 1, 1988, the ASPCA notified the mayor of New York that as of July 1, 1990, it would no longer collect the New York City dog license fees (this amounted to twenty-two months' notice, four months more than the amendment required). Thereafter, if the city wanted the ASPCA to provide animal control services, it would have to negotiate a separate contract with the society to provide full funding for the requested services. The city quickly discovered that no other organization was ready or willing to enter into such an agreement to provide the needed services, so it agreed to contract with the ASPCA to provide animal control services. The terms of the contract provided funding to capture stray animals and hold them for the prescribed three days, to hold and observe dogs who had bitten people for ten days, to euthanize unwanted animals, and other similar activities. The contract did not provide funding to operate an adoption program or spay/neuter services for the public. These were considered nonessential humane services, and the ASPCA would need to fund these from its charitable donations.

The society's ability to absorb a budget deficit at this time was severely limited by financial commitments it made with bondholders to fund the construction of a new headquarters building half a block away on Ninety-second Street, and a new animal shelter at East 110th Street. The society's longtime practice of supplementing inadequate funding for animal control through deficit spending was no longer an option. It would risk defaulting on the bonds that were issued. The new headquarters was completed, as was the new shelter. The ASPCA moved to those locations in late spring of 1992.

Many details, large and small, are involved in moving a complex organization from one place to another. Not surprisingly, one detail fell through the cracks. At closing, when it was time for the ASPCA to turn its vacated facility over to the developer who had purchased the property, an attorney directed the society to give the new owner a key to the building. Key? What key? No one seemed to have a key. For forty years, someone had always been on duty at the ASPCA. The door was open all day, and at night, there was a doorbell to ring, and someone from the night shift would open the door to receive animals from the public, firemen, and policemen. Whatever keys existed had been long lost, and no one bothered to have copies made. Why would they? The ASPCA was always there. But to complete the legal transfer of the property, a quick call to an overnight locksmith produced two brand new, unused keys for presentation to the building's new owners.

In 1991, as the ASPCA approached its 125th anniversary, it struggled with its identity and its role in a rapidly evolving animal protection movement. It did so under a dangling sword of Damocles—the constant concern about funding for animal control programs. Contractual funding from the city became the new worry. As the City Council wrestled with the mayor over a budget, vendors waiting to be paid for "services rendered" often were left absorbing the costs for months at a time. The ASPCA worried constantly that payment might not arrive and further service cuts would need to be made, or, worst case, that the animal control program would be suspended completely. John Kullberg left the presidency in 1991, and was replaced by Roger Caras. The former broadcast journalist, author, and naturalist inherited an organization celebrating 125 years, but with an uncertain future.

In 1992, the ASPCA received $4.5 million from the city to run animal control services. The society supplemented that figure with an additional $1.5 million. Negotiations with the New York City Department of Health to renew the contract did not go well. Research completed by ASPCA staff indicated that while most major cities provided animal control funding at the rate of two to three dollars per capita, the City of New York rate came to just fifty-six cents per person. Presentation of these data did little to garner increased support. In fact, the ASPCA was asked to absorb a *reduction* in funding. A series of meetings between ASPCA board members and senior staff led to a momentous board meeting in March 1993. Seated beneath a portrait of ASPCA founder, Henry

Bergh, the board debated the merits of continuing to provide animal control services for the City of New York. Before the night was over, the board had voted unanimously to notify the city that the society would not renew its contract to provide animal control services. On March 24, 1993, Caras addressed a packed press conference making the announcement public. In reporting the story, the *New York Times* wrote that the ASPCA's decision was both philosophical and practical—practical in that being perceived as dog and cat killers made it very difficult to attract donations, and philosophical in that "it's a nightmare to kill 30,000 to 40,000 animals a year. That's not our mission."

The message the ASPCA sent to the city stipulated that the ASPCA would continue to operate the shelters until December 31, 1994, and would work with the city until that date to develop an alternative service option. The city's initial reaction was to threaten legal action that would compel the ASPCA to continue to provide animal shelter services. That strategy failed, however, thanks to the amendments to the 1894 dog license law. Next the city sent out a Request for Proposals to a number of the local animal groups that had been critical of the ASPCA's perform-ance, as well as to other groups across the country. But no group was willing or able to provide the full range of services that were required, at the level of compensation that the city was willing to pay. Eventually, the city formed the Center for Animal Care and Control (CACC), a new nonprofit entity. The CACC would provide the city's animal control services, and it would be under the city's control.

The transition to the new system was rocky. Even though the ASPCA offered substantial help with the transition, hard feelings limited the extent to which city officials and new management at the CACC were willing to accept that help. Local activists who had been jubilant when the ASPCA announced that it would no longer run the city animal shel-ters were soon divided over how the city should proceed. More than anything, people were struck with the bitter reality that thousands of unwanted animals would still be euthanized in the shelters each year. Many had assumed the animals died because the ASPCA did not care. The transition process now helped to clarify that the problem was mamm-moth and the resources meager.

The transition was further complicated by one final controversy from this period involving the ASPCA. On January 21, 1994, the *New York Post* trumpeted the headline, "Puppygate!" An internal audit at the ASPCA revealed that for several years a number of kennel workers had been able to manipulate the system used to assign overtime, resulting in six-figure incomes for themselves. Several members of the senior administrative staff were implicated in the scandal. They were suspended and then discharged. Fortunately, the society's budget was able to withstand the drain.

As part of the transition, the ASPCA turned over the two shelters that it was operating in Brooklyn and Manhattan, as well as three pet-receiving centers that it had established in Queens, Staten Island, and the Bronx for part-time services. At the close of business December 31, 1994, facility and program management at the five locations was transferred to CACC staff, ending the ASPCA's one-hundred-year stint at handling animal control for New York City.

Chapter 4

Horses and Farm Animals

Had it not been for the horse, there might be no ASPCA, for it was the mistreatment of this "most noble servant of mankind" that first and so powerfully outraged Henry Bergh's sense of justice. Bergh was in Russia when he discovered that he could take effective action to protect horses from abuse. Back home in New York City, he was constantly confronted with the plight of the horse, who was both ubiquitous at the time and increasingly ill suited to living and working conditions in the city as the population on the narrow island of Manhattan exploded in midcentury.

The horse was absolutely essential to the commercial life of New York City in 1866. Horses pulled sleds and lorries and wagons of every sort and for every purpose. They pulled railroad cars full of people and they pulled fire wagons full of water. They pulled wealthy people's carriages and working people's carts laden with goods, produce, and smaller animals on their way to slaughter. North of the city, horses and mules pulled barges along hundreds of miles of canals. The economy of the entire region was linked to the horse, yet they were overloaded, overdriven, and overworked until they collapsed in the street, whereupon they were beaten in an attempt to get them back on their feet. Horses unable to rise were left to die where they fell, however long it took. Injured, lame, sick, and old horses who couldn't work were turned out into the street and allowed to starve to death. The streets themselves, particularly those covered with the slippery, uneven surface called "Russ pavement," were dangerous in the extreme, accounting for disabling injuries to 1,500 horses a month. It was the enormous disjuncture between how much humanity owed to the horse and how little it gave back to them that compelled Bergh to found the ASPCA.

Not surprisingly, Bergh's very first attempt to enforce the new anticruelty law involved a man beating his horse. Although the society's president had the new law in his pocket, he succeeded only in getting
laughed at and challenged to duke it out in the street. Fortunately he was
to have many more successes than failures in the months ahead. Perhaps
because horse abuse was so common, or perhaps because it was a sight
that especially disturbed him, Bergh chose a scene that depicted this form
of cruelty for the ASPCA's official seal. The image he selected had
appeared on the front cover of *Frank Leslie's Illustrated Newspaper* a full six
months before the society was founded (Leslie was a founding patron). It
shows a horse in traces who has fallen. Above the terrified animal looms
his owner, with a cart rung held high in striking position. Behind the
horse stands an angel with the sword of justice in one hand and the other
hand raised in solemn warning: *This must cease.*

Three bronze castings were made of the seal. One hangs in the
ASPCA's headquarters building. One is on Bergh's grave in Green-Wood
Cemetery. The third is on the grave of Louis Bonard, the French fur
trader who admired the society's work and left most of his money and
real estate to the society, making him the ASPCA's first major donor.
Bonard's grave is also in Green-Wood Cemetery.

Although Bergh stated on more than one occasion that it was justice,
not sentiment that motivated him to devote his life to protecting animals,
some who knew him thought that he did have a special feeling for the
horse. He is said to have worn a cravat pin adorned with a horse's head.
Even more revealing, Bergh actually kept some horses at his country cottage on Lake Mahopac, north of New York City. A correspondent to
the *Herald* sent this report from Lake Mahopac in the summer of 1871:

When Colonel Frine, the Peruvian Minister, first saw Mr. Bergh's private horses,
he said he was never more astonished in his life. He expected to see fine, spirited
animals, whereas he gazed upon great lean, rawboned beasts, exactly like the
stage and car horses of New York City. Doubtless Bergh bought them through
pity.

Throughout Bergh's tenure as president, the ASPCA's annual reports
were filled with arrests and convictions of people who beat and otherwise
abused their horses. The report for the year that Bergh died summarized
the society's work with horses since its founding. It listed horses disabled
past recovery and humanely destroyed: 26,554; horses temporarily disabled and suspended from work: 36,857; and disabled horses removed
from the streets by ambulance: 4,939. The same annual report noted that

progress was being made with regard to the city's railroad horses. Apparently a better class of animals was being used, with double teams available in winter, and water and shelter stations distributed along the railroad routes in summer. It concluded with this comment: "It is to be hoped that the coming year will find in the electric motor, or cable, an effectual substitute for horses as a propelling power."

This did not occur in the coming year, but eventually it did come to pass. Yet even when horses had largely disappeared from the streets of New York City, they continued to be a special interest of the ASPCA. The city still has a carriage-horse trade, primarily as a tourist attraction, and in 1989 the ASPCA led the fight to regulate this tiny but powerful industry by limiting the number of hours the horses work, setting limits on the extremes of temperature in which they may work, and restricting their work to the less congested streets of the borough. Unfortunately these regulations expired in 1994, and conditions for the horses worsened again. The society has fought to restrict the horses' work area to Central Park, and to provide them with turnout areas in the park, and improve the stables where they are kept, but the society has been unable to get the new proposal introduced in City Council. Just as in Bergh's day, the city is an inhospitable place for horses. The ASPCA's humane law enforcement agents do inspect the horses for properly fitted harnesses and fitness to work. In 2007 one officer was assigned to monitor the city's carriage horses full-time.

During the years when horses were the society's primary focus, many important innovations were made on their behalf, not the least of which was the horse ambulance in 1867 and a horse sling that could be hooked to a winch to raise a horse who had fallen into the river or an excavation. Ten elaborate water fountains were built in a variety of locations throughout the city, and where there were no fountains, hundreds of water troughs were placed. In later years, when the fountains and troughs had all been removed because horses for the most part had disappeared, the ASPCA carried water in a truck during the hot weather for the several hundred carriage horses and other novelty horses who remained. On November 21, 2001, one of the old water troughs was rededicated in a public ceremony and placed in Grand Army Plaza at the entrance to Central Park, where it is being used again by the city's carriage horses and the Parks and Recreation Department's mounted units. The trough had served horses for decades before being retired in 1955 and returned to the ASPCA.

In 1933, ASPCA board member Alfred Maclay donated a trophy for a junior riding championship, to be awarded each fall at the National

Horse Show in New York City. Among the qualities the competitors are judged on is humane treatment of their mounts. The ASPCA still presents this trophy every year.

In 1996 the ASPCA set up the Lucky Fund, named for a so-called "Premarin® foal" named Lucky, who was rescued by the ASPCA and placed at Green Chimneys, a residential farm and school north of New York City where at-risk youth and abused animals are enabled to heal one another. Monies from the Lucky Fund were used each year to purchase a number of Premarin foals who otherwise would have gone to slaughter. The Lucky Fund, renamed as the Equine Fund, helps horses in a variety of ways, from bringing food and water to wild horses in drought-stricken areas to helping reputable horse-rescue organizations handle emergencies or increase their capacity. Hundreds of horses have been saved and placed in good homes with the fund's assistance.

The ASPCA helps save and care for countless horses all over the country through its quarterly Equine Fund grants. In 2006, it awarded $125,000 in grants, and is looking to double that amount in 2007. Equine Fund grants are issued to organizations focused on saving horses impacted by the hormone-replacement industry, wild horses and burros, and those in need of rescue from abuse, neglect, unfortunate circumstances, and the slaughter auctions. The ASPCA works with grantees to determine the best application of funds, and 2006 saw grants being used for a wide range of initiatives: to improve rescue facilities and expand or renovate physical structures, to promote humane messages through training and education, and to provide lifesaving sustenance during periods of drought. Several grants supported population control efforts, including one that utilized immunocontraception for herd management of wild horses.

The ASPCA's legislative team has been active on both the state and federal levels in lobbying for legislation to protect all American horses from slaughter for human consumption overseas, particularly the wild mustangs and burros in the West who are so much a part of our history.

Some of the first cruelty cases that Henry Bergh prosecuted were for the mistreatment of livestock and other animals on the way to slaughter. Perpetrators were stunned, convinced that Bergh's contention that animals should not have their legs tied and be stacked like cordwood was born of a foolish, soft heart, and would make it impossible for them to do a profitable business. Newspapers of the day took this as just one more opportunity to mock Bergh. How or why should animals with just days or moments to live extract an obligation from the men tasked with their demise? Bergh stood fast. He argued that of all animals, those who would soon give their lives to sustain humanity were most deserving of kindness until their last moments.

Bergh and the ASPCA were among the leaders in the formation of the American Humane Association, a national body that represented humane groups from across the country. The groups effectively campaigned for enforcement of a "28 hour law" that required that all animals being shipped be allowed food, water, and some exercise after twenty-eight hours in transit. Enacted in 1873, this law set an important precedent in the nineteenth century, as most long-distance transport was by train, moving cattle from western plains and feedlots to eastern markets. It was also among the first federal laws established to protect animal welfare. Unfortunately it was something of a high watermark for the following century. While little happened at the national level, ASPCA agents continued to perform inspections of live poultry and meat markets in New York City, and would frequently write summonses for substandard conditions or mistreatment of the animals.

In the years that followed, humane slaughter was one of the most compelling issues pursued by the ASPCA and other humane organizations. While treatment of animals at local live markets could vary tremendously, the relatively small size of these facilities made inspection and subsequent improvements relatively easy to accomplish. As the United States' economy changed and small markets were replaced by larger supermarkets, it became more and more difficult to monitor conditions at slaughter. Instead of live animals being shipped to neighborhood butcher shops—where they would be slaughtered one at a time, and then butchered for sale—large numbers of animals were shipped to large slaughterhouses and packing plants where hundreds, and indeed thousands of animals were killed each day and processed for shipping as whole carcasses, halves, or quarters. Slaughter at these assembly-line facilities could be chaotic and inhumane to both the animals and the workers. Upton Sinclair's *The Jungle*, published in 1906, depicted the horrific conditions in the Chicago slaughterhouses. His revelations led to some improvements. However, the need for a federal standard for humane slaughter remained on the national animal welfare agenda.

By 1955, a number of improvements in slaughter methods made it possible to introduce a bill requiring the use of humane slaughter methods, specifically, rendering animals unconscious before their carotid arteries were cut. The national campaign to promote the bill mobilized the efforts of more than five hundred humane groups from around the country. The ASPCA helped to lead the way by printing and distributing pamphlets, mailing out press releases, and sending representatives to

Washington to testify at hearings before the Senate Agriculture Committee. Congress finally passed a humane slaughter law in 1958, and it was signed by President Dwight D. Eisenhower. This law made it mandatory for all meat purchased by the United States Government to be humanely slaughtered beginning July 1, 1960. The law did not cover all animals brought to slaughter or all slaughter facilities and companies. However, since many meat packers wanted to retain their supply contracts with the federal government, and it was not economical to maintain two different types of slaughter equipment, most of these packers converted to acceptable humane methods. As a result, up to ninety percent of the meat purchased in the United States was processed through humane methods as prescribed by the law.

Several individual states passed additional legislation that required humane slaughter for all animals within the state. In the 1960s, the ASPCA worked with the New York State Humane Association to pass legislation in New York to cover all animals slaughtered for food. Movement on the New York State bill was thwarted by several factors. First, the State Department of Agriculture wanted to observe how the recently passed federal law was implemented. The more prominent concern, however, was that five different bills were presented for consideration in New York State. They differed in several ways, but the most important distinction among the various bills was whether Orthodox Jewish ritual slaughter, which involved hoisting conscious animals into the air upside down to bleed out without being "contaminated" by the blood of other animals on the slaughterhouse floor, would be included or exempted from the law. The federal law exempted ritual slaughter from its provisions. In New York State, where there was a high percentage of kosher packing houses, this provision was a make-or-break issue for passage of a law. State legislators, seeing that humane advocates were divided over the humane slaughter issue, declined consideration of a bill until there was some agreement among the advocates. The ASPCA supported a humane slaughter bill that exempted kosher slaughter, believing it better to get something in place, even if not a perfect bill.

While legislation was considered, the ASPCA pursued a practical approach. In 1963 the society purchased the rights to a large-animal slaughter pen that was both humane and met the requirements of kosher slaughter. The pen had been developed by Cross Brothers of Philadelphia and George A. Hormel Co., and the ASPCA provided the plans free of charge to any packing houses willing to convert to the system. The ASPCA also committed $200,000 to the development of a small-animal slaughter pen. The industrial design firm of Raymond Loewy/William

Snaith was commissioned to design and develop a prototype device for restraining the animals without the need to hoist them by the leg, thus allowing them to be slaughtered in a natural upright position. Initial testing was done at Cornell University, and final field testing under slaughterhouse conditions at the College of Agriculture and Home Economics at Ohio State University. The ASPCA made a concerted effort to ensure that the resulting device would be acceptable to the Jewish community. The ASPCA consulted with the Rabbinical Council of America, the Joint Advisory Committee of the Synagogue Council of America, and other groups representing the interests of the Jewish community. The final device was both humane and did win the acceptance of orthodox rabbis for kosher slaughter. The device is still in use today, and variations of it are promoted by Dr. Temple Grandin, an author and associate professor at Colorado State University who is well known for her contributions to humane slaughter around the world.

The ASPCA's continued commitment to farm animal welfare is now reflected in its support for Humane Farm Animal Care (HFAC). From its inception, the ASPCA has supported HFAC with financial contributions, and by having staff and board members serve on the HFAC board of directors, science advisory committee, and as field inspectors. Headquartered in Herndon, Virginia, HFAC is the first organization to establish standards for the humane treatment of farm animals, from birth to slaughter, accepted by both the United States Department of Agriculture and the International Standards Organization. These standards were based on a similar program developed by the Royal Society for the Prevention of Cruelty to Animals in England. They were modified and expanded by a science advisory committee that includes many of the most respected farm animal welfare scientists and professionals in the United States.

Producers who apply to participate in the HFAC program are inspected by a trained, independent inspector. The standards are specific for each species, but include a nutritious diet without antibiotics or hormones, shelter and resting areas for the animals, and sufficient space to be able to engage in natural behaviors. Producers who meet the standards are authorized to place the "Certified Humane Raised and Handled" sticker on their meats, eggs, or dairy products. Farmers pay a royalty to HFAC for the right to use the sticker label, and support promotion of the program. All facilities are inspected on an annual basis, and are required to keep extensive records on the health and well-being of their animals. Inspectors note any deficiencies in the farm's practices or conditions, and these must be corrected to earn or retain the right to label their products as "certified humane." Established in 2003, HFAC has certified more than sixty farming operations in the United States and Canada. Products bearing the seal include eggs, milk and cheese, ham and bacon, pork, beef, lamb, veal, turkey, chicken, and more. In the program's first year, 143,000 animals were raised under certified humane standards. In 2006, the number had risen to more than 14 million.

In 2007, Adele Douglass, a former American Humane Association staff member who single-handedly created Humane Farm Animal Care and serves as its executive director, was named a finalist in the second annual Purpose Prize Awards, a program that invests $100,000 in each of five Americans over the age of sixty who are solving some of society's most pressing problems in what normally is considered their retirement years.

Chapter 5

Pets and People: The ASPCA's New Mission

Protecting horses and livestock made perfect sense in 1866. These animals had *value*. Dating back to the Mayflower Compact, laws and regulations reflected that, if nothing else, these animals needed to be protected due to their value as property. People depended on livestock and especially on horses for many of life's necessities. Not so with dogs, cats, and other small animals. Henry Bergh's arguments for forming the ASPCA and passing the 1866 animal cruelty law acknowledged the important role that horses and livestock played in the economy. Protecting dogs and cats, however—well, that smacked of pure sentimentalism. Undeterred, Bergh went ahead full bore to protect *all* the "brute creation."

Early ASPCA annual reports include examples of Bergh intervening to protect dogs, cats, and other animals from cruelty. Few dogs in the 1860s received the pampered treatment that millions do today in our homes. Unrecorded numbers roamed the streets of the city, scratching out an existence while presenting a risk to public health and safety. Brewers, butchers, and other merchants used horses to pull their wagons, as did the trolley car companies of the day, but people at the bottom of the economic ladder could not afford the upkeep of a horse to transport their meager goods and help them ply their trade. Thus rag pickers, who salvaged and resold the fabric from discarded clothing, depended on dogs to pull their small carts. These canine beasts of burden were themselves a ragtag lot. Lured into service with a tempting morsel, the dog was turned loose at the end of a hard day of work to scavenge a meal on the streets. Some wandered back the next morning, expecting another bit of food.

Some dogs were employed to run alongside horse-drawn wagons to protect the horse, wagon, and contents while deliveries were made. The

Dalmatian, a breed that had been developed overseas in the mid-eighteenth century to run with horse carriages, attained iconic status in America as "the firehouse dog." They attained this nickname for their instinct to dash beside the powerful draft horses who answered the alarm bell and raced in hitch to haul the fire wagon to the site of a blaze. A century and a half later, this image is perpetuated in the award-winning advertisements of Anheuser-Busch that feature their world-renowned team of Clydesdales pulling a bright red wagon, always with a proud Dalmatian perched on top.

Other working dogs of the day included so-called turnspits. Most of these were small terrier mixes who ran inside stationary wheels, similar to those used today to exercise pet hamsters and gerbils. The wheels were connected by gears to the rods, or spits, suspended over fire pits. As the dogs turned the wheels, the spit rotated, and with it the roasts and poultry being cooked over the fire. In an era before spaying and neutering became a common and accepted practice, all the various and sundry dogs of the city were able to contribute their progeny to a surging population of homeless street animals.

The population of strays made working dogs a cheap commodity, easily replaced by others. Unless a dog was especially skilled, or trained for a particular task, there was no reason to invest in feeding and caring for the dog. It was easier, and cheaper, to lure another off the street when needed. The canines that received the best care were the better fighting and ratting dogs. They were athletes, and their performance, and progeny, were valued.

While pet keeping was not as common as today, it was a well-established practice. In her 2006 book, *Pets in America: A History*, Katherine C. Grier documented the fact that both rich and poor kept a wide variety of different animals as pets. Dogs were certainly a dominant theme, but cats had their aficionados as well. Dogs and cats were supplemented by small songbirds, mammals, reptiles, and fish. Sailors and other travelers frequently returned from their journeys with small monkeys, parrots, or other exotic souvenirs. Journals, letters, and other documents of the era confirm that people kept pets in the mid-nineteenth century for the same reasons we do today: for companionship, for fun, to show off to friends and neighbors, and as a source of pride.

Most different from today, however, was the do-it-yourself nature of acquiring a pet. It was not unusual for people to catch pets from the wild. Birds, baby squirrels, raccoons, and other animals were all popular choices. At a time before radio or recorded music, small caged birds provided cheerful background sound for lonely farmhouses and cramped city apartments. In the 1800s, the first commercial dog and cat foods were being developed. Diets were still largely homemade and consisted of left-overs and table scraps. Finding veterinary care at the time was a hit-or-miss proposition. For the most part, veterinarians treated horses and livestock and had limited experience or training in the ailments of dogs, cats, and other small animals. All this would change rapidly in the years ahead.

Since 1877, dog lovers across the United States, ranging from the most dedicated breeder or fancier to those whose interest is casual, have turned their attention to New York City's Madison Square Garden. For two days in February, the Westminster Kennel Club dog show attracts tens of thousands of fans in person, and many millions more to its live broadcast on television. Westminster is one of the nation's oldest dog shows and inarguably its most prestigious fixture, drawing many of the top dogs in the world. When the show was first held in 1877, the dog fancy—dedicated breeders and exhibitors—was just getting organized in America. Following the example being set across the Atlantic, a small group of fanciers was determined to formalize its passion for dogs and settle the question of who bred and owned the finest specimens, and which dogs' genes should influence the future direction of the various breeds.

While Henry Bergh often intervened on behalf of mangy street curs, his personal pedigree made him well accepted among the doggy set, almost entirely made up of wealthy people at that time. Already recognized for his efforts on behalf of animals, he was tapped to be the keynote speaker at the first Westminster Kennel Club show. Whether many in attendance at the show actually heard his words is doubtful. Accounts of the evening attest that he was in competition with a full-throated chorus of barks and howls. Unlike today, the canines at the show had not been accustomed from an early age to the close proximity of unfamiliar dogs. The record states that Bergh praised the quality of both the people and the dogs at the historic event. He noted that such wonderful representatives of the canine race could only come from people who truly understood and provided for their welfare. He also pointed out that not all dogs were so fortunate as to receive the care and attention lavished upon those present.

It would appear that at least this part of Bergh's message struck fertile ground, for the organizers of the show voted to bestow profits from the event upon the ASPCA. The amount of $1,297.25 was forwarded to Henry Bergh, for the intention of funding a "home for stray and disabled dogs, similar to the one in London." Bergh, ever conservative with money and careful with his plans, was gracious in expressing his thanks. Knowing that the amount provided was not sufficient for the task, he indicated that he would hold the money for the intended purpose until all of the needed funds were in hand. (The following year, mindful of how noisy the previous show had been, Bergh sent a letter to the managers of Westminster rather than deliver a speech that few could hear.)

A century after Henry Bergh addressed Westminster, another ASPCA president did the same. Roger Caras, the society's fourteenth president and a prolific author and well-known broadcaster about animals, was for many years the "voice of Westminster." As such, his task was to introduce each breed to the packed arena and viewers at home during the two successive evenings of Variety Group judging. Caras, a member of the elite Westminster Kennel Club, always urged his listeners to obtain their dogs from responsible breeders. But when he became the ASPCA's president in 1991, he added that they should also consider adopting a dog from their local shelter—"or better yet, get one of each!"

Throughout their parallel histories, there have been numerous instances of congruence between the ASPCA, representing shelter dogs, and the world of the purebred dog, as embodied in the American Kennel Club and, in New York City at least, by Westminster Kennel Club. Large numbers of ASPCA members and supporters have owned and enjoyed registered purebreds as well as shelter dogs and dogs of mixed breeding. Additionally, a number of individuals have served as officers and board members at both organizations.

Westminster in 1877 was a glimpse of what life could be like for many dogs in America. In New York City, however, the more common fate was that of a furtive stray dashing up to a cart to steal a fallen sausage or pawing through a pile of trash for a scrap to eat. While some dogs were already enjoying the status of pampered pets and were given formal funerals when they died, the majority met their fate in an iron cage on the East Side of Manhattan. When the city pound was full of unwanted animals, they were loaded into an iron cage, hoisted up by a derrick, swung out over the East River, lowered into the swirling waters, and drowned. If Bergh was excoriated for his efforts to protect horses because doing so interfered with commerce and owners' rights to do as they wished with their own property, his railing against the treatment of homeless dogs and cats at the city pound drew scorn for misplaced sympathy and concern. These animals were a blight upon the city—what possible issue should Bergh or anyone else have with their treatment or manner of demise?

Bergh persevered, and his ongoing criticism, widely published in the city's newspapers, eventually drew public support for his point of view. In the end, the city administration called upon Bergh and his society to take over the running of the city pound. Even though the city offered to pay for this work, Bergh demurred. He knew well the politics and people involved—this was the heyday of William M. "Boss" Tweed and the infamous Tammany Hall political machine—and Bergh did not trust them to keep up their end of the bargain.

In the mid-1800s, dog catching was a tawdry and corrupt practice. Dog "pounds" had evolved from the livestock impounds that developed during the early days of the colonies. At that time, most households kept their own small flock of chickens for eggs, a goat or a cow for milk, and perhaps a so-called feeder pig, fattened on kitchen scraps for later slaughter. Animals who escaped and wandered off were captured by the town "pound master" and taken to the local impound. Owners could redeem their animals by paying a redemption fee. Animals who were not reclaimed by their owners became the property of the pound master. The pound master could either sell the animal or keep him or her and slaughter him for his own use. The pound master made his living through redemption fees, selling some unclaimed stock, and keeping others to feed his own family.

Dogs and cats also wandered about the towns but were usually tolerated unless they became a nuisance. If the pound master knew the owner of a particular dog, he might catch and hold the dog until the owner came to reclaim his animal and pay a redemption fee. It would be rare for someone to buy one of the unclaimed dogs or cats. It was easy enough to just catch a stray. At the same time, cultural prohibitions prevented the pound master from selling the dogs or cats he might have for slaughter. In the end, most of the small animals were killed in the most convenient fashion. Shooting was costly and dangerous, so clubbing and strangling were not uncommon. Drowning, as done in New York City, was an option where bodies of water were readily available.

In large cities like New York, where livestock and other animals were less common, dogs and some cats were the pound master's primary stock in trade, with redemption fees being his main source of income. Since catching homeless strays was hard work and was not likely to provide much compensation, many pound masters resorted to a form of extortion. They would literally steal a dog from an owner's yard, and then inform him that his dog was at the pound and would be killed unless he paid a redemption fee. Some owners resorted to paying "protection" money to the pound master in exchange for his not kidnapping their dogs. In places where the pound master was paid per head for each dog caught, he might resort to importing dogs from outside the community in order to increase his head count, and hence his income.

In addition to being subjected to Bergh's unrelenting public criticism of the pound, the city also had to deal with the "Great Meddler's" more direct attentions. In the society's annual report for 1880, it was stated that the city's dogcatchers needed constant supervision, and that several had been arrested for cruelty. It was problems with corruption as much as the mistreatment of the animals that led the city to call upon the ASPCA again and again to take over the dog pounds. In 1894, six years after Bergh's death, the ASPCA board finally agreed.

When Bergh began his work, he was very much in the streets, stalking the people who were breaking the animal cruelty law. Accounts from these early days do not mention taking animals into custody for care. In many cases, horses were destroyed to prevent further suffering. Dogs and cats who were rescued from various predicaments were either returned to their owners or set free.

By 1867, the society began to operate its first ambulance for injured horses. (New York's Bellevue Hospital, founded in 1811 and credited with being the first human hospital in the world to put a corps of ambulances on the street, did not trot out its first conveyance until two years later.) The society's first ambulances of course were horse drawn, and an ambulance house was acquired. Injured horses and others deemed unfit for work were transported by ambulance either to the owner's stable or to another location where they could receive care. In time, however, some rescued dogs and cats were brought to the ambulance house, which gradually became a de facto shelter for these small animals. As the number of ambulances increased, so did the space needed to park them and to house the horses who pulled them through the city. These locations were the first animal shelters operated by the ASPCA. In 1891, the ASPCA introduced an ambulance for small animals.

When the ASPCA agreed to take over the city pound in 1894, it was the first time that an SPCA or humane group was officially designated to fulfill the "animal control" needs for the city. On March 8, 1894, the governor of New York State signed a bill that authorized the ASPCA to issue dog licenses and renewals; return lost dogs to owners; seize unlicensed dogs and any cats without identification; maintain shelters for lost, stray, or homeless animals; and provide a painless death for unclaimed animals or animals who were not placed with new owners. In the nineteenth century, in the days before rabies vaccines for animals, large numbers of dogs and cats running at large were a considerable threat to the public health, and so-called animal control was thus a responsibility that local governments took on in the interest of protecting people, not out of concern for the dogs and cats.

In the twenty-first century, more and more animal-control departments have added "care" to their names, and do have the best interests of
stray and unowned animals at heart. Still, the fact that these agencies normally are subsumed within a city's health department indicates that their
first responsibility is still the public health. In New York City today, for
example, the animal care and control function is lodged within the
Department of Health and Mental Hygiene. However, the mission statement of Animal Care and Control of New York City is "to promote and
protect the health, safety and welfare of pets and people." Pets come
first!

Henry Bergh was autocratic, and while he lived, the ASPCA board
followed his lead. His focus on enforcing the anticruelty law precluded
any substantial effort to develop animal shelters in New York City. Thus,
in 1874, the first humane animal shelter was founded in Philadelphia by
the Women's Branch of the Pennsylvania SPCA under the leadership of
Carolyn Earle White, a frequent correspondent with Bergh. Named the
Morris Refuge Association for Homeless and Suffering Animals, the shelter picked up stray and injured dogs and cats and took in unwanted animals. The shelter was designed to be sanitary, and the dogs and cats were
fed wholesome food and provided with medical care if needed. Owners
were able to reclaim lost pets, and others were able to adopt a dog or a
cat. Animals who were seriously injured, sick, not reclaimed by their
owners, or not placed in a new home, were destroyed in a humane
euthanasia chamber that the Women's Branch had commissioned. Animals placed into the steel box were asphyxiated by an introduced gas. In
keeping with the spirit of reform that was sweeping the nation, the first
humane shelter for animals pointed the direction for the future, and was
a completely different undertaking than a municipal pound.

Horses were beginning to be replaced by other modes of transportation
at the end of the nineteenth century, and the ASPCA gradually turned
more of its attention to dogs and cats. Henry Bergh had died in March
1888, and in 1894, the ASPCA agreed to manage animal control for the
city. For the next one hundred years the ASPCA would struggle to meet
this enormous commitment that strained its budget to the breaking point,
while trying to maintain a high enough level of public support to keep
the doors open. The ASPCA did this through its animal hospital, which
offered excellent care to the community's animals for a reasonable price,
or in hardship cases, for free. It also did it through visible efforts to prevent cruelty on the city's streets, through its humane education programs
that went into the schools as well as brought groups of scouts and students on field trips into the society's headquarters building, through

obedience training classes for the public, and other programs. Yes, the ASPCA was the city's dogcatcher, but it was a lot more, too. And of course the ASPCA's shelters were always a source for nice family pets. Many thousands of unwanted animals were euthanized every year, but there was always a ready supply of dogs and cats, puppies and kittens.

After World War II, more and more people became pet owners, and the pets were gradually becoming family members rather than guard dogs or rodent-catching machines. Many factors contributed to this phenomenon, which has continued unabated to the present time. From the thirties through the fifties, first motion pictures and then television programs starring animals helped feed the new interest in having a pet like the one on the screen or like, as Patti Page's 1952 hit record suggested, "the doggie in the window." As pets in large numbers started to move indoors, it became important to keep them brushed and bathed, and grooming shops flourished to meet the need, especially of the small purebred dogs with long coats such as the wildly popular poodle. Families even began to take their pets with them on vacation. The ASPCA began to provide pet owners with practical information on pet care, including the need for annual vaccinations.

Even though pets were becoming more and more a focus for the ASPCA, the welfare of other animals was still the society's "business," too. In 1958, the ASPCA opened an innovative facility at Idlewild Field in Queens (later to become John F. Kennedy International Airport) to provide services for animals being transported by air. The Sydney H. Coleman Animalport, named for a former general manager of the American Humane Association and subsequent senior executive of the ASPCA, was modeled on a similar facility operated by the RSPCA in England. It was located on 1.25 acres of land and cost over $500,000 to construct. The building was roughly 5,000 square feet and included sixty kennels, cages, and adjustable box stalls. The stalls could be configured to hold everything from sheep and goats to horses and cattle and even elephants and giraffes. Large sliding doors allowed transport trucks to drive right into the facility to permit the safe loading and unloading of animals. A modern veterinary clinic was on-site to provide everything from basic examinations and care to surgery, if needed. It employed multiple-zone climate controls so that polar bears and tropical birds would be equally comfortable.

The Animalport was open seven days a week, twenty-four hours a day. A resident manager and his wife lived on-site and were available at all times to assist with animals being transported through the airport. People who were traveling with their pets could drop their animal off at the Animalport when they arrived at the airport. ASPCA staff gave dogs one last walk before putting them back into their shipping crates, and then delivered them to the plane for loading just before the plane left the gate. If staff were notified of pets on arriving flights, they met the plane, supervised unloading, and transported the pets back to the Animalport, where they received a quick exam, some water, and exercise. Once pet owners had gathered up their baggage, they headed over to the Animalport to pick up their companions. In the early years of the Animalport's operation, ninety percent of the dogs arriving from overseas belonged to servicemen returning to the United States from military duty abroad. Airline and animal professionals alike hailed the benefits of the Animalport.

Zoo curators, especially, were pleased to have the often-rare specimens they were expecting get the red-carpet treatment at the Animalport. In the days before sturdy commercial air shipping containers, many animals were shipped to the U.S. in jury-rigged crates made of wooden slats and chicken wire. More than once these containers broke open during flight, and ground crews who opened the cargo hold were greeted by a chattering flock of parakeets or a troop of furious monkeys. That led to an urgent call to ASPCA Animalport staff, who clambered through the hold with net and lasso to round up these errant passengers.

In addition to zoo stock, many animals destined for stage and screen moved through the Animalport. The U.S. Equestrian Team used the facility when shipping their mounts overseas for Olympic competition. The special caging and food-preparation areas at Animalport also made it a convenient and safe location for holding some of the more unusual animals that ASPCA agents or rescue crews came across in their work. Each year, a couple of lions turned up in the city, along with chimpanzees, sheep, goats, monkeys, and other creatures.

Because it was off the beaten path on the airport grounds, Animalport had few curiosity seekers show up to peek in on some exotic guest. On the other hand, many of the city's news photographers and film crews were in on the Animalport's location. A call from the ASPCA's Public Relations department would usually guarantee a photo session and an appearance on the evening news or in the next day's newspapers.

Regular boarders at the Animalport included the USDA's Beagle Brigade. These small hounds are trained to examine incoming baggage for the presence of contraband vegetables, fruits, or other agricultural products that could harbor pests or diseases that might prove harmful to American crops. Beagles are chosen for this duty because of their superior scenting ability and a generally cheerful demeanor unlikely to rouse fear or concern among arriving passengers.

ASPCA staff at Animalport provided direct care to animals being transported by air, but they also conducted regular training sessions for airline personnel on the proper care and handling of animals being shipped. The presence of the ASPCA at the airport provided the society with an intimate look at the problems associated with the air transport of animals. In January 1974, the ASPCA hosted a meeting at the International Hotel near the airport to address some of these issues. Among the groups attending were the United States Departments of Agriculture, Health, and the Interior; the Port Authority of New York and New Jersey; and the New York City Department of Health. The groups discussed areas of overlapping authority as well as areas where regulations fell short in providing adequate oversight.

During the years that Animalport was in existence, the ASPCA published a booklet called *Traveling with Your Pet*. It was a listing of countries and their entry requirements for companion animals. The booklet was revised a number of times until the ASPCA was no longer able to provide the staff and financial resources necessary to ensure that it was accurate and up to date. The last edition was published in 1988.

Until Animalport was closed in 1994, the society played a significant role in protecting animals being shipped by air. Several factors drove the decision to close the facility. Economics was one. The companies that regularly shipped horses built their own facility, eliminating income from that source. In the early 1990s, concern about Ebola virus resulted in a significant reduction in the import of monkeys from overseas, further reducing a source of income. The final blow came when the Port Authority decided that the Animalport would need to be moved in order to accommodate upgrades and expansion of the airport. Negotiations between the ASPCA and the Port Authority for a new location at the airport, including compensation for the loss of the capital investment in the existing facility, did not produce a satisfactory agreement, and the facility was closed.

Throughout the thirty-six years that it was in operation, Animalport was a boon to the Port Authority and the City of New York. To have a facility at the airport that could safely and professionally accommodate everyone from a single individual traveling with her family pet to professional organizations shipping large and valuable exotics gave the city bragging rights not available to other metropolitan areas. Only two years after Animalport closed, the city's image was tarnished when "Boris," a pit bull mix, escaped from his in-flight-damaged kennel upon arrival at New York's LaGuardia Airport. Delta Airline cargo handlers, untrained and unknowledgeable in animal handling techniques, gave chase, but the terrified dog ran out of the terminal building and melted into the densely populated neighborhood around the airport. When the dog's frantic owner approached Delta for help, she was handed a lost-baggage claim form, and dismissed.

Boris was located six weeks later, filthy and emaciated, but alive, about two miles from the airport. But the story did not end there. The ASPCA's Government Affairs National Office in Washington, D.C., worked closely with Boris's owner and key legislators to draft and introduce legislation that would offer greater protection for pets being shipped by air. The so-called "Boris Bill" eventually became the Safe Air Transport for Animals Act, and went into effect in June 2005. Nevertheless, in February 2006, a prized show dog named Vivi, who had just been shown at the Westminster Kennel Club dog show, escaped her kennel at Kennedy Airport, giving rise to an all-out search that involved Port Authority and airlines personnel, animal communicators, and hundreds of volunteers from the community. While the new Safe Air Transport law mandates training for airline personnel who handle animals, the training either wasn't done or wasn't adequate to develop the skills needed to prevent Vivi from bolting out of the airport—skills that the ASPCA's Animalport staff had possessed in great abundance.

When the ASPCA announced that it would no longer provide animal control services for New York City, it emphasized its intention to remain active in the city, expanding its law enforcement program and spay and neuter services. It would also reestablish its national presence by expanding its outreach activities. So, as it closed the doors of the shelters on the last day of 1994, it opened new doors on the future.

First of these new doors was the establishment of a Shelter Outreach department. The department began with a single staff member, Julie Morris. Morris was already a professional shelter director who "had the good fortune" to do postgraduate study under Professor John Paul Scott in 1976–1977. She credits the "undisputed father of canine behavior studies" with influencing her choice of a career in animal welfare. Under Morris's leadership, Shelter Outreach eventually grew into a department of more than thirty, with a wealth of skills and centuries of combined experience in animal sheltering. Shelter Outreach staff became popular speakers at animal sheltering conferences across the country, providing lectures and workshops on topics ranging from kennel cleaning and sanitation to strategic planning and board development. Staff visited many local shelters across the country to provide mentoring and advice as needed on facility and program management. As the department grew, regional managers were appointed in different parts of the country to keep track of each area's unique needs.

The Shelter Outreach department resurrected two earlier programs—Adopt a Shelter Cat Month and Adopt a Shelter Dog Month, in June and October, respectively. These programs enlisted the support of corporate sponsors to enable hundreds of animal shelters across the country to participate in shared promotions encouraging the adoption of homeless animals. The Shelter Outreach department also became a conduit for corporations to provide grants and support to local shelters. The network of connections developed through sponsoring and speaking at national and regional conferences—combined with the many personal visits regional managers made to animal shelters—resulted in an exceptional system for evaluating the needs of the sheltering community, and then directing hundreds of thousands of dollars in grants to places where they would be most useful.

Several of these grants provided unexpected dividends. With financial support from pet food manufacturer Iams, a grant to the Kansas Humane Society of Wichita led to the development of Meet Your Match™, a system that matches potential adopters with available dogs in a shelter. Under this program—developed by Emily Weiss, Ph.D., certified applied animal behaviorist—dogs available for adoption are given behavior evaluations, and people looking for a pet complete a questionnaire about their lifestyle and what they are looking for in a dog. They then receive a color-coded pass that directs them to the dogs in the kennel who are most likely to match their expectations. Additional funding from Iams allowed further development of the concept, and it has now been rolled out to shelters across the country. Dr. Weiss has since joined the ASPCA, and with other staff from the department, has gone on to develop a version of the program to support cat adoptions.

Several years after the establishment of the Shelter Outreach department, a Veterinary Outreach department was created to develop and promote the field of animal shelter medicine. Lila Miller, D.V.M., an experienced ASPCA shelter veterinarian, wrote articles, delivered lectures, and consulted with local animal shelters and veterinarians on the unique elements of practicing veterinary medicine in the animal shelter environment. In the late 1990s, Cornell University invited Dr. Miller to develop the first course in animal shelter medicine at a veterinary college. The course debuted in 1999 and has been offered as an elective every spring semester since then, with enrollment growing from an initial group of seven students to a typical class of twenty-five to thirty students each year. As interest in the field developed, Veterinary Information Network (VIN), a major provider of online continuing education credits for veterinarians and veterinary technicians, asked the ASPCA Veterinary

Outreach department to develop an online introduction to the field in 2003. A second online course on disease management in animal shelters was added in 2004, and a course on the role of the veterinarian in investigating animal abuse was added in 2005. In many ways, the field was "officially" born as an academic discipline with the publication of *Shelter Medicine for Veterinarians and Staff* in 2004. Edited by Miller and Stephen Zawistowski, the volume includes thirty chapters contributed by recognized authorities on topics ranging from the history of animal shelters to vaccination protocols and veterinary forensics. It rapidly gained acceptance as a text used at veterinary colleges across the country, and as a must-have resource for animal shelters requiring authoritative information.

The ASPCA Veterinary Outreach department expanded in 2005 by adding a shelter veterinary expert in spay/neuter and pediatric surgery, Leslie Appel, D.V.M. This added expertise has been instrumental in allowing the ASPCA to provide information and training to promote the use of credible and proven pediatric and high-quality, high-volume surgical techniques in both community and shelter spay/neuter programs. These programs target populations that are unlikely to utilize conventional veterinary services due to inaccessibility or cost and thus contribute to the surplus of unwanted animals.

The department now offers shelter medicine lectures at several veterinary colleges and at the major veterinary conferences, in addition to animal welfare groups and individual shelters. Dr. Miller initiated a shelter medicine externship program at the ASPCA headquarters for third- and fourth-year veterinary students. The program focuses on medical and behavior programs for animals in shelters, animal welfare issues, mobile spay/neuter programs, and how to conduct an animal-cruelty investigation. This popular and well-received program has contributed to veterinary students' choosing shelter medicine as a career.

As Americans became more and more inclined to think of their pets as family, it became obvious that the death of that family member was a significant event that much of society was not yet fully acknowledging. The ASPCA Counseling department was formed in May 1992 to help meet this issue head-on. Paula Anreder, M.S.W., joined the society to provide help to people confronting pet loss and dealing with grief. Anreder made frequent forays to the waiting room of the Bergh Memorial Animal Hospital to comfort pet owners whose pet had just died, or who were struggling with the difficult decision to euthanize a pet with a serious illness or injury. Word of the program soon spread, and veterinarians across the city were referring clients in the throes of grief to the

ASPCA Counseling program. Anreder juggled telephone calls, letters, and private visits with grief-stricken pet owners to offer help and support in a time of need.

The breadth of the program soon expanded. Shelter staff—individuals who came to the ASPCA because they loved animals—were overwhelmed and lost in their jobs dealing with the stress of people relinquishing their pets, caring for dogs and cats who often had been neglected and ill-treated, and ultimately euthanizing hundreds of animals. Anreder soon developed discussion meetings for ASPCA shelter staff, and met with individuals to help them work through the stress of a job that required care and concern for animals, and too often forced them to confront neglect and cruelty. Word of Anreder's success in doing this work at the ASPCA soon spread beyond New York City, and in April 1993 she was invited by the Rhode Island Foundation to conduct a workshop, "Stress in the Workplace." Animal shelter staff attended to learn about a number of significant but generally ignored topics in animal welfare at that time: How to deal with the human side of euthanizing homeless animals, how to deal with an irresponsible public that abandons healthy animals, and how to support people who are grieving over the death of a beloved pet. For the animal care profession these issues have jelled into a concern dubbed "compassion fatigue."

Paula Anreder's service to the ASPCA and further development of this field were cut short by her illness and untimely passing in 1996. Dr. Stephanie LaFarge, a psychologist, took over the Counseling department in March 1997. Dr. LaFarge extended the reach and role of Counseling into some new and different areas. She reestablished a connection with the Society for the Prevention of Cruelty to Children (SPCC), the agency Henry Bergh cofounded in 1874 but with which the ASPCA had had little contact for many years. Working with SPCC and a variety of other groups throughout New York City, including the Administration for Children's Services and the New York Police Department, a series of meetings were held under the umbrella name of NYC Family VISION (Violence Intervention, Sharing Information and Observation Network). These informational meetings allowed participants to discuss shared goals and concerns. The general topic of domestic violence was the core of these meetings, and all participants understood that violence in the home could be directed at children, partners, elders, and pets. ASPCA staff, including humane law enforcement officers, helped to train field staff from other agencies in how to recognize and report animal cruelty.

LaFarge has also assisted with the further development of ASPCA Pet Therapy programs and currently serves on the board of directors of the

Delta Society, an organization based in Washington State that was founded in 1977 to investigate and promote the health benefits of animal-human interactions. She continues to provide pet-loss counseling, and is currently working with the veterinarians at the ASPCA Animal Poison Control Center in Urbana, Illinois, to develop skills helpful when dealing with distressed pet owners over the telephone.

Beginning in 1995, the ASPCA was redefining itself as an organization. No longer burdened with the financial strain of New York City's animal control program, it was able to invest in new programs and approaches to its original mission of preventing cruelty to animals. Money and resources were directed to humane law enforcement, education activities, federal and state legislative work, national shelter outreach, and mobile medical and adoption units to bring services to underserved areas in the city. Progress was steady, but slow. It would take time, especially in New York City, for the public to understand that the ASPCA no longer did animal control, which to most people meant killing animals. Entirely by accident, two national tragedies propelled the "new" ASPCA into the spotlight: first to New Yorkers, and then to the nation.

On September 11, 2001, terrorist attacks on the World Trade Center in New York City and on the Pentagon in Virginia brought America and the world to a standstill. While most people were powerless to do more than watch television and pray, within hours of the collapse of the World Trade Center in lower Manhattan, ASPCA staff and vehicles were rolling south from headquarters to rescue pets from apartments around "Ground Zero." Larry Hawk, D.V.M., president of the ASPCA at the time, led one of the teams. Emergency supplies were quickly loaded into the mobile medical van that normally brought spay/neuter services to impoverished city neighborhoods. In addition to the medical van, the ASPCA convoy included several law enforcement vehicles and uniformed agents. Roadblocks across streets leading to Ground Zero kept most people out of danger and out of the way, but ASPCA agents were recognized as law enforcement professionals and were permitted to escort the ASPCA convoy into the area. As Dr. Hawk moved into position with the team, he learned that his sister, a flight attendant for American Airlines, had been on the American Airlines jet that struck the North Tower. He put his grief aside for the moment and went to work with the other veterinarians, technicians, and agents helping to rescue and treat animals in need.

Back at ASPCA headquarters, the boardroom quickly was converted into a command center. Calls poured in from the public about pets who needed to be rescued from apartments near the crash site. Headquarters staff relayed the information to the team at Ground Zero. ASPCA staff from all departments rallied to the task. Technical staff jury-rigged phone systems and computers to take the calls and create databases to keep track of animals who had been rescued and then brought to the ASPCA hospital or into kennels that were cleared in the shelter. Other staff volunteered to clean cages or care for animals, since animal care staff scheduled for later shifts that day were unable to get to work due to roadblocks, closed bridges, and suspended mass transit.

ASPCA agents were permitted to enter zones prohibited to nondesignated responders. They were allowed to escort owners to retrieve their pets, or when necessary, enter apartments alone to collect dogs, cats, turtles, birds, and goldfish left behind when people went to work that day. There was no electricity, so each trip involved multiple flights of stairs in darkness, and a trip back down with a terrified pet.

The constant news crawl at the bottom of television screens throughout the disaster included an 800 number for pet owners to call the ASPCA with information on animals that needed to be rescued. Hawk and other ASPCA staff appeared on various newscasts with updates on the animal rescue efforts. Eventually two hundred animals were rescued and returned to their owners, and within a week of the attacks, the ASPCA had provided care for more than five hundred. People who thought that the ASPCA had abandoned the animals of New York by not renewing its animal control contract, saw that the ASPCA was still there, ready to protect the city's pets in new ways.

The work of the ASPCA did not end with the rescue efforts. A Family Assistance Center was established on a pier in the Hudson River. At first this was the designated location for people to come to report missing family members and friends. Photos and descriptions of missing persons were posted on walls in the center. Eventually, the center became the place where family members came to request expedited death certificates for those lost, bringing in hair samples that would later be used for DNA identification of any remains that were found. The Red Cross set up tables and a kitchen to provide meals and areas where rescue workers from Ground Zero could rest. Concern about pets who were still missing resulted in a request for an ASPCA presence at the Family Assistance Center. Dr. LaFarge, who is a Delta Society–certified pet therapist as well as a pet-loss counselor, headed the society's team. Reports of lost pets and requests for rescue were accepted and relayed to the ASPCA command center at headquarters. Eventually the ASPCA's role grew and evolved. Volunteers from various pet therapy groups, including the Delta Society and Therapy Dogs International, offered their services to provide a calming and therapeutic intervention for devastated family members and exhausted rescue workers alike. Managers at the Family Assistance Center asked Dr. LaFarge to coordinate and validate the credentials of pet therapy teams. More than three hundred pet therapy teams volunteered at the center before the operation closed.

Teams were effective in a variety of ways. They might sit with a group of children as mom, dad, or another relative met with a caseworker who assisted with necessary paperwork. Some of the work was heartbreaking, some of it heart lifting. Children would talk about their mom, who worked in one of the towers, and how much she liked dogs and cats, asking if there would be dogs and cats in heaven. Rescue workers would come in, still coated in dust and dirt from working on "the pile." Many had recovered the bodies of fellow firemen or police officers. It seemed that the words they could not share with colleagues were whispered into the ears of therapy dogs who came to greet them.

The ASPCA's role during 9/11 attracted the attention of people in New York and across the country. It brought to the ASPCA a new constituency that saw the organization not as the New York City dog-catcher, but as one that responded effectively in a time of need.

The second tragedy occurred on August 29, 2005, when Hurricane Katrina roared across the Gulf of Mexico and slammed into the United States Gulf Coast. This time New Orleans was ground zero. First it was battered by 100-plus mph winds, torrential rain, and a storm surge projected at twenty-eight feet. As the hurricane passed, experts began to make their initial assessments of the damage. It seemed the city had narrowly escaped disaster. But hours later, three levees that protected the city gave way, and vast areas were inundated. Thousands of people were now stranded, often with their pets. Many other pets had been left behind when people had evacuated ahead of the storm.

The ASPCA, along with other national and local animal groups, quickly responded to undertake animal rescue operations. Once again a command center was established at the ASPCA to gather information on pets who were lost, people who wanted to volunteer with hands-on rescue, and still others who wanted to donate money to help with the crisis. Eventually, thousands of pets were rescued, and provided with food, water, and medical care. Once they were stable, they were moved into foster care with shelters and rescue groups across the country until they could either be reunited with their original families or placed in new homes.

Now the national network developed by the Shelter Outreach department bore fruit. Shelters were contacted to provide help with rescue, equipment, and holding space to foster animals. Once again staff from across the organization stepped up to do any job that was needed. The communications team worked around the clock to keep the ASPCA Web site updated with the most recent information available on the situation. Development and accounting staff did yeoman work processing the millions of dollars in donations now flowing into the organization. Shelter Outreach staff took turns rotating through the disaster zone to help with rescue work and on-site sheltering and shipping operations. ASPCA veterinarians and veterinary technicians deployed to help with medical care for animals. A team from New York drove one of the ASPCA mobile clinics from the city to New Orleans, where it was used to support rescue operations. The van took a beating on the debris-strewn roads in New Orleans. Staff scavenged tires and other parts from abandoned vehicles to keep it running. When operations eventually ended, the van was donated to a local group. Possibly the most appreciated of the ASPCA's contributions to the effort were the checks it put in the mail to support local groups coping with the disaster. As the public opened its hearts and wallets to the Gulf Coast's animals, the ASPCA quickly converted that generosity into the supplies and aid needed to support the shelters and people in the field.

In the aftermath of Hurricane Katrina, the ASPCA was recognized and praised for its integrity during the rescue operations, and the skill and dedication of the staff that deployed to the region. The recovery work in New Orleans and elsewhere on the Gulf Coast will take years to complete. The ASPCA committed millions of additional dollars, expertise, and other resources to help local shelters rebuild and renew themselves.

Hurricanes Katrina and Rita (in August and September 2005 respectively) made it obvious that a coordinated disaster-response program was needed at the national level. The ASPCA, the Humane Society of the United States (HSUS), the Society of Animal Welfare Administrators, veterinary groups, and others held a series of meetings to examine what went right and what did not work so well during the response to Katrina. Memoranda of Understanding (MOUs) were drafted among the various groups to establish protocols for disaster response, basic training required for direct response, and other needs.

As part of the national effort, the ASPCA established a Disaster Readiness department. The department focuses on both preparation for disasters and on direct response, with trained staff ready to perform animal rescue under potentially dangerous conditions. Information for the public and communities emphasizes such things as having an evacuation plan in place for family pets that includes a "crash bag," containing food, water, medical and identification information, extra leashes, and other necessary items.

Several teams of ASPCA staff have undergone extensive training for technical animal rescue. When a disaster strikes, these teams go on alert, ready to deploy where their skills are needed. These skills include swift-water rescue, rappelling, and ice rescue, among others. While no one is eager for another disaster on the scale of Katrina, teams and associations are in place to ensure that animals will receive the best attention possible. In addition to training its own staff, the ASPCA has partnered with the Sacramento, California–based United Animal Nations (UAN) to provide disaster readiness and rescue training across the country. Volunteers who complete the training will be able to join the UAN Emergency Animal Rescue Service (EARS), and receive the credentials required for deployment to a disaster zone.

Concurrently, the ASPCA Legislative Services team lobbied for and helped pass the federal Pets Evacuation and Transportation Standards (PETS) Act, signed into law by President Bush in October 2006. On the state level, the team spearheaded passage of comprehensive legislation in Louisiana and Illinois requiring disaster evacuation plans to include pets. It helped achieve similar laws in California, Florida, Hawaii, and New York.

Also in 2006, the ASPCA completed a major renovation of its shelter. Designed to boost adoptions, the $5 million expansion and renovation involved 12,000 square feet on two floors. On the lobby level, the Onyx and Breezy Shefts Adoption Center, named for two black Labrador retrievers, now has sixteen large glass enclosures for dogs, six community cat rooms, and twenty-four individual cat habitats. On the fourth floor, 19 dog and 112 cat habitats have replaced what used to be office space. The center can now house up to 350 cats and dogs on any given day.

Cages are gone, replaced by pet-friendly features such as glass condos, cozy beds, the use of noise-reducing materials, piped in "dog laughter" and bird songs, and ten to twelve daily air exchanges that keep air fresh and limit the spread of disease. Portals allow cats to move from one unit to another, and knee-level "scent holes" in glass-fronted dog pens allow canines to sniff visitors and accept treats. Spacious playrooms allow dogs to romp and play. Together, these and other improvements create a less stressful environment for pets and a more inviting space for visitors who are thinking about adoption.

People who work at the ASPCA benefit from the "no-kill" environment and all the enhancements to the lives of the animals in the society's shelter. The ASPCA has always attracted compassionate individuals who truly care about animals. Staff at all levels are involved with the ASPCA's mission. Office workers and executives walk dogs and foster undersocial-ized cats and dogs in their offices. Many staff members adopt pets from the ASPCA or other rescue facilities throughout the city.

Knowing how many of the society's employees have rescued pets, the ASPCA's president came up with the idea of featuring some of those pets—and people—on the organization's calendar. The ASPCA *Companions for Life* calendar launched in 2002. For the Direct Response team, this was a great opportunity to really set the ASPCA calendar apart from all the other fund-raising calendars out there. Ordinarily, organizations design their own calendars but illustrate them with "stock" photography. The Companions for Life calendar allows the ASPCA to give its donors a glimpse of the personal commitment and generosity that ASPCA employees have shown through their choice to rescue a homeless animal. The calendar combines striking photographs and true stories of wonderful pets adopted by ASPCA staff across the organization. The first three cal-endars were shot by renowned New York City–based pet photographer Kim Levin. In 2004 Kim had a baby, and could not allocate the time or the resources to shoot the calendar. When the word circulated that a new photographer was needed, ASPCA executive vice president and chief of operations, Steve Musso, passed on the contact information of his wife's close friend, accomplished fashion photographer and animal lover, Jack Deutsch. Although Deutsch had photographed nearly everything *but* ani-mals in his thirty-year career, he was interested in taking on the chal-lenge. Deutsch has been shooting the calendar ever since (with the exception of 2006, when the ASPCA marked its 140th anniversary with a "heritage" style keepsake calendar), and believes that the patience and perseverance he's had to cultivate in order to get great animal portraits has made him a better photographer.

The ASPCA calendar is mailed to an average of 500,000 current donors and members every year, and of course everyone who works for the society has the current edition hanging in their work space. The calendar serves as a morale boost for ASPCA employees and volunteers, who are tremendously proud to see their own special furry friends grace the pages of a nationally distributed calendar.

Chapter 6

Veterinary Services

W hen Henry Bergh introduced the horse ambulance in 1867, it revolutionized the care of injured horses. It also meant that the ASPCA needed to have on hand its own stable of horses to serve as engines of mercy, pulling the ambulance wherever needed throughout the city. The ambulance horses needed regular care, so the ASPCA began to enlist the services of veterinary surgeons. These veterinarians provided care not only for the ASPCA's horses, but also for some of the horses who were picked up in the ambulance. The society did not operate a hospital at this time, so the horses were treated at the ambulance house where they were stabled.

Veterinary medicine was just developing as a formal, science-based profession at this time, with a substantial amount of the care and treatment of horses being provided by farriers, the blacksmiths who shoed horses. There was also a number of frank quacks and untrained, self-styled "horse doctors" offering their services to the public. On several occasions, ASPCA agents needed to step in and issue summonses or arrest individuals who were doing more harm than good to the horses under their care.

Henry Bergh was deeply concerned by the lack of professional standards of veterinary practice. In the society's annual report for 1877, he lamented the absence of any accredited college in the state to certify the knowledge and credentials of veterinarians, stating that "every hostler, whose experience has never extended beyond the confines of a stable or a blacksmith's shop, is permitted to practice on horses and other animals a series of the most diabolical tortures." Bergh went on to call for legislation to rectify the situation.

Meanwhile, Bergh had enlisted one of the leading veterinarians of the day to make sure that the society's horses suffered no such torture. French-trained Dr. Alexandre F. Liautard, who founded the American

Veterinary College in New York City in 1875 and was an elected officer of the nascent American Veterinary Medical Association, was one of two veterinary surgeons listed as officers of the society in 1877. Liautard did as much as any individual to bring about the improvements in education and training that Bergh found so urgently needed. In a *New York Times* article headlined "Horse Doctors No More," published on April 19, 1891, Bergh and his associates at the ASPCA were credited with helping to elevate the veterinary profession by first engendering humane feelings toward animals:

These men were the first to advance the argument that a sick horse or a sick dog should be treated, not by ignorant blacksmiths or stablemen, but by men who knew as much about the diseases peculiar to the animal as did the regular physician of diseases peculiar to man.

In fact, so poor was the reputation of the horse doctor before specialized schools were established, that people who owned thoroughbred horses or purebred dogs were much more likely to call in a medical doctor than an animal doctor if one of their valuable charges required treatment. Eventually states passed laws that made it illegal to practice veterinary medicine without being certified by an accredited institution.

By 1912, the demand for more space and updated facilities resulted in the ASPCA's completing work on a new ambulance house at Twenty-fourth Street and Avenue A on New York's East Side. This new location included an animal hospital. At first, it was dedicated to the care of horses and featured a variety of innovations that facilitated the movement and treatment of injured equines. Slings, ramps, tilting tables, and overhead tracks simplified the difficult process of moving horses from the ambulances to the treatment areas.

ASPCA veterinarians soon became recognized for their equine expertise, especially their ability to diagnose and treat major injuries. During the first World War, ASPCA chief veterinarian, Dr. George W. Little, prepared and delivered a series of lectures entitled "Horses in Warfare," and on hippology, or general horse care, for the Army Corps. In gratitude, the Army presented Dr. Little with a memorial cup acknowledging and thanking him for his patriotic service.

Additional veterinary services in the city were provided by the New York Women's League for Animals. This group, originally formed as the Women's Auxiliary of the ASPCA, had become the Women's League for Animals in 1910. In 1914, the league opened its own animal hospital on Lafayette Street on Manhattan's Lower East Side. This would eventually become the renowned Animal Medical Center, one of the premier veterinary facilities in the United States, which moved to its present location on East Sixty-second Street in 1961.

Another of the society's early veterinarians was Dr. Samuel K. Johnson. He worked at the ASPCA hospital, but also served as State Veterinarian and had an office where he saw private clients. One day in 1896 a woman came to his office with an unusual problem. Her dog had died at home, and she wanted to give her pet a proper burial. Even then it was illegal to bury an animal in Manhattan. After pondering the situation, Dr. Johnson offered a solution. He owned a cottage in Hartsdale, a sleepy community about an hour north of the city. On the property was an apple orchard. If the woman could transport her dog to Hartsdale, the doctor said, she could bury the animal in his apple orchard. The woman gratefully accepted. A short time later, Dr. Johnson happened to relate this story to a friend who was a reporter, and was surprised a few days later when the account appeared in print. Soon he was besieged with similar requests from the owners of other deceased pets. Eventually Dr. Johnson's apple orchard became Hartsdale Pet Cemetery, the first cemetery for animals in the United States. The cemetery has been in continuous operation to the present day.

For more than one hundred years, pets from all walks of life, including exotics, have been interred at Hartsdale. In addition, the nation's first memorial to "war dogs" was installed at Hartsdale. This monument, which consists of a bronze sculpture of a German shepherd dog wearing a Red Cross blanket, was established in 1923 to honor the dogs who had served in World War I. Annual ceremonies are held at Hartsdale on Memorial Day to commemorate the contributions of military dogs in all succeeding conflicts.

Although originally designed to treat horses, the ASPCA hospital soon began to provide care for dogs, cats, and other small animals. There were few veterinary practices at the time that offered care for pets, so the ASPCA hospital rapidly became a popular option for people who needed this service. Infectious diseases such as distemper and rabies were still a scourge, and the need to isolate animals placed a strain on the hospital's resources. Meanwhile, the range of illnesses and injuries seen by the hospital staff caused the ASPCA to be at the forefront of developments in veterinary medicine. In 1920, the society acquired its first X-ray machine, ushering in a new era for diagnostics and treatment. In 1921, the hospital began to treat animal cancers with radium, staying apace of developments in medical care for humans. As the caseload for the hospital continued to grow, it was clear that more space was needed, and in 1925 the facility was expanded for the first time. Then-Chief Veterinarian Dr. Raymond Garbutt also expanded the ASPCA's outreach to the public by initiating a series of weekly radio lectures on animal care. In 1927, an extensive renovation provided the hospital with new isolation wards for the treatment of distemper and infectious skin conditions like sarcoptic mange.

From its earliest days, the ASPCA hospital provided care for animals belonging to both the financially secure and the poor. For those who could afford the fees, the ASPCA hospital offered excellent care at a reasonable price. However, for those who did not have the means to purchase professional treatment at a private veterinary practice, the ASPCA was often the last and only hope for treatment. In most cases, the clients were asked to pay what they could. Sometimes this would be just a few dollars. Other times a payment plan was offered. Never was this option more needed, or more appreciated, than during the years of the Great Depression. When many people were unable to afford medical care for themselves, the ASPCA provided care for their animals. In 1932, seventy percent of the animals seen at the ASPCA hospital were charity cases. This placed a tremendous burden on the society, since these years also saw a decline in the membership fees and private donations that were necessary to supplement the income derived from treatment fees.

When the society was forced to vacate its facility at Twenty-fourth Street and Avenue A after World War II, plans for the new headquarters included a modern animal hospital. The new hospital opened with two surgical suites, five examining rooms, a treatment room, pharmacy, and an X-ray and fluoroscope room. Soon after opening, a $60,000 expansion provided a pathology laboratory. Many of the new pieces of equipment were financed by contributions of ASPCA members and supporters during the capital campaign to complete the new facility. The hospital staff had expanded to include a director, an office manager, nine veterinarians, nine attendants, a laboratory technician, porter, night supervisor, and five office staff. Regular clinic hours were from 9:00 A.M. to 4:30 P.M., Monday through Saturday, with emergency hours until 7:00 P.M. each day. Patients were seen on a first-come, first-served basis, although appointments to see a specific veterinarian could be booked for a small additional fee.

In addition to outpatient service at the clinic, the society also operated an ambulance service for the public. In an emergency, or if the client was unable to bring in her animal herself, the hospital could dispatch an ambulance to pick up the pet. Ambulance service was available twenty-four hours per day, with the fee dependent on the distance traveled. The ambulances were staffed by trained personnel and were equipped with an oxygen tank, stretcher, emergency lights, and first-aid kit.

The hospital operated on veterinary medicine's cutting edge. Sanitary and aseptic conditions were practiced. Examining and operating tables were sterilized after each patient. Kennels and outdoor runs were disinfected daily. Surgeons "scrubbed up" with antiseptics before an operation, and wore face masks and gloves during the procedure. The new hospital included a contagious ward to isolate infectious patients from the balance of the hospital population. The veterinary staff continued their research into the treatment of cancers of pets. In cooperation with the Memorial Sloan-Kettering Cancer Center, they conducted research on tumors and other growths in dogs. Tumor specimens were sent from the ASPCA to Sloan-Kettering where they were examined by the pathologists. Using the results of these examinations, ASPCA veterinarians were able to adjust their diagnosis and treatment of the growth. A variety of new anticancer drugs were being tested as part of this effort. Clients at the ASPCA hospital paid an initial diagnostic fee, and those animals thought to be appropriate for treatment received the balance of their care in the hospital free of charge. Results of the treatment were shared with the doctors at Sloan-Kettering, where the same drugs were being tested on humans. This close cooperation between the ASPCA hospital and Sloan-Kettering advanced the care and treatment of both human and canine cancer patients. In 2007, the American Medical Association (AMA) voted to increase collaboration with the American Veterinary Medical Association (AVMA) in pursuit of "one medicine," a nineteenth-century concept that has been rediscovered in the twenty-first.

The new hospital facility also allowed the ASPCA to initiate a veterinary internship program. While an internship was not required for a licensed veterinarian who had completed his studies and passed his boards, many graduates were interested in obtaining some additional experience before hanging up their shingles. The advantage to the ASPCA was to bring in young veterinarians with the most up-to-date information on animal diseases, surgical techniques, and various veterinary procedures and practices. The interns were also cheap labor—the annual salary in the early 1970s was just $7,500!

There generally were seven interns at any one time, and they came from veterinary colleges across the country. The number of interns was intentional, since each young doctor took a turn on the night shift each week to ensure that a qualified veterinarian was available at all times. The interns were exposed to the entire spectrum of veterinary practice while at the ASPCA. The high volume of clients who came to the hospital, in addition to the animals who came through the shelter or were rescued by the society's humane law enforcement agents, afforded the interns the opportunity to work on everything from infectious diseases, injuries, foreign body ingestion, urinary obstructions, so-called high-rise syndrome (cats falling out the open windows of apartment buildings), dogfight bites, and gunshot wounds—to name just a few. Many of the interns saw more cases and a greater variety of cases in their year at the ASPCA than they did while in veterinary school or later in formal residencies elsewhere.

During this era, there were few internship opportunities available for graduating veterinary students. As a result, competition was stiff for the handful of spots available at the ASPCA. That meant that the ASPCA was able to attract the best and brightest to the program. In the end, both the ASPCA and the interns benefited, and perhaps the veterinary profession, as well. Quite a few of the former interns have gone on to highly successful careers in the field. A number have been successful practitioners, playing important roles in the various veterinary societies, including the American Animal Hospital Association, the American Veterinary Medical Association, and local organizations. Others have gone on to distinguished careers in academia, conducting research and training new veterinarians.

ASPCA veterinary alumni attest that their time at the ASPCA had a significant influence on their careers and the development of their thinking on animal welfare and veterinary medicine. This is not surprising. The entrance to the hospital and the shelter in Manhattan were through a common lobby. Interns coming to work walked past the front counter for the shelter, where people were relinquishing unwanted pets or looking for lost ones. A ramp led up to the hospital on the second floor, and walking to the ramp took the interns past the window of the display area where puppies were available for adoption. They also would have known about the 100,000 or more dogs and cats being euthanized at the shelter each year.

Dr. Phil Bushby is just one veterinarian who benefited from the ASPCA internship program and found it had a lasting impact on his career. He was an intern from 1972 to 1973, and then a surgical resident from 1973 until 1974. He later went on to a surgical residency at Auburn University, and eventually became a board-certified veterinary surgeon. He is now the Marcia Lane Endowed Professor of Humane Ethics and Animal Welfare at the Mississippi State College of Veterinary Medicine. For the past fourteen years, he has taken students to area shelters to perform spay/neuter surgeries and learn about how shelters operate and their unique medical needs. Fate brought Dr. Bushby and the ASPCA back together in the months and years following Hurricane Katrina in 2005.

He is now a key player in the recovery plan for the Gulf Coast region, and is an important factor in efforts funded by the ASPCA and other animal welfare groups to ensure that rebuilding in the region includes badly needed veterinary services, especially affordable and readily available spay/neuter programs.

By the 1980s the internship program had been discontinued. Several factors contributed to its demise. A number of other internship opportunities had been developed, so demand for the spots at the ASPCA declined. At the same time, the financial stress that the animal-control program placed on the organization made it difficult to support the interns. The cost of living had increased to the point that it was no longer possible to find young veterinarians willing or able to scrape by on the meager salaries that the ASPCA was able to allocate to the program.

A brief externship in shelter medicine was established in the late 1990s. Still in existence, it is a summer program for veterinary students, lasting just one month. The externs are provided with a small stipend and given broad exposure to the wide range of ASPCA activities. They spend time in the animal shelter helping with examinations and vaccinations. They observe behavior evaluations of animals for adoption, learn about behavior rehabilitation and training, travel on the mobile spay/neuter adoption van, meet with humane law enforcement investigators, and participate in humane education presentations. Many of these young people intend to pursue careers in animal welfare when they complete their veterinary studies. Several of the early participants in the program have already gone on to work at animal shelters.

In 2006 the ASPCA reintroduced its internship program. Once again, recent veterinary graduates are welcomed to the ASPCA hospital to develop their medical skills and their interest and commitment to animal welfare.

The ASPCA's relationship with the veterinary profession dates back to the 1870s. In June 2007, the society set down on paper the current breadth and depth of this association. The document highlights the services the society has to offer to the profession, both locally and nationally, and its own credentials in veterinary medicine that support its bid to be recognized as an important resource.

ASPCA services to veterinarians include consultation and referrals on spay/neuter programs; on cruelty cases, including veterinary forensics and training veterinarians how to give courtroom testimony; and on shelter medicine issues, including one-on-one consultation with a shelter veterinarian. The ASPCA Animal Poison Control Center (APCC) offers a 24/7/365 emergency hotline and a toxicology residency in collaboration with the University of Illinois College of Veterinary Medicine. Veterinary clinics that subscribe to the free APCC Veterinary Lifeline Partner Program™ (VLPP) enjoy not only expedited processing of their poisoning cases but receive benefits that include three free Registry of Approved Continuing Education online sessions yearly for their staff, and a quarterly e-newsletter. Through its Animal Behavior Center, the ASPCA offers consultations on behavior for veterinarians. Additionally, in the Champaign-Urbana area, the center provides veterinarians with a place to refer their clients for an in-home consultation for pets with behavior problems. Finally, at the Bergh Memorial Animal Hospital (BMAH) in New York City, the ASPCA offers six one-year veterinary internships, where doctors rotate through internal medicine, surgery, dermatology, humane law enforcement, shelter medicine, general medicine, and emergency service. The BMAH also offers short (one- to three-week) externships for veterinary students.

There are fifty-four veterinarians on staff at the ASPCA, including twelve board-certified toxicologists at the APCC. ASPCA veterinarians contribute to the profession by serving on the committees of American Veterinary Medical Association and of veterinary specialty colleges; by working as adjunct faculty at veterinary colleges for toxicology and shelter medicine; and by providing continuing education in shelter medicine, toxicology, veterinary forensics, behavior, dermatology, and other topics at local, regional, and national conferences. ASPCA staff have served as editors of the first-ever text on shelter medicine and are in the process of preparing a second. Others have written a text on veterinary forensics, and they have developed courses on shelter medicine, spaying and neutering, and forensics for veterinary schools. APCC veterinary staff alone have written eighteen peer-reviewed journal articles and forty-seven book chapters, advised the Environmental Protection Agency on veterinary language for pesticide product labels and, based on case data, provided critical information on national animal poison issues, most particularly during the pet food recall crisis of 2007.

Henry Bergh would be pleased indeed with the extent to which his society has advanced knowledge in the field of animal health. Not surprised, but pleased.

What is now the ASPCA Animal Poison Control Center began life as the brainchild of Dr. William Buck, a renowned veterinary toxicologist. In the early 1970s, while at the University of Iowa, Dr. Buck often consulted on animal poisoning cases with former students, and with veterinarians from around the state. As word spread of his expertise and willingness to help, the number of calls began to increase, so he drafted his graduate students into helping with the calls. He subsequently took a position at the University of Illinois College of Veterinary Medicine at Urbana. In the fall of 1978, Dr. Buck and his graduate students at the University of Illinois inaugurated the Animal Toxicology Hotline when they began to handle calls around the clock using a paging service. The only expense to the caller was the actual telephone call itself.

Initially, the service focused on handling cases from within the state of Illinois. But when the hotline number was broadcast on a national radio show and appeared on the label of a popular rodenticide, the number of calls from outside Illinois increased, and in 1980 the name was changed to the Animal Poison Control Center. In 1984, reflecting the scope of the center's work, its name was again changed, this time to the National Animal Poison Control Center.

Veterinary toxicologists and students manned the telephone service in shifts to provide coverage twenty-four hours a day, seven days a week, 365 days a year. Eventually the cost of managing the service exceeded the veterinary school's ability to subsidize all expenses, and a fee of thirty dollars was instituted. Callers, who now included members of the public, could pay the fee with a credit card, or by calling a 900 number that automatically added the fee to their telephone bill.

In 1995, despite the fees it was charging, the center remained in financial trouble. It needed to upgrade the telephone system and its computers. It was also squeezed for space within the confines of the veterinary college. The university gave Dr. Buck permission to seek additional outside assistance. When Dr. Buck approached Arco Chemical Company, one of the corporations that contracted with the center to provide postmarketing surveillance on its products, a happy coincidence occurred. Arco was also a corporate partner of the ASPCA, jointly promoting a propylene glycol-based antifreeze that is less toxic to animals than antifreeze made of ethylene glycol. Arco contacted staff at the ASPCA, suggesting that a meeting between the National Animal Poison Control Center and the ASPCA might prove productive. That was indeed the case. In August 1996, the ASPCA signed an agreement with the University of Illinois to acquire the National Animal Poison Control Center. After a brief transition period, the center was renamed the ASPCA Animal Poison Control Center and moved to a new location off-campus, but still near the university in Urbana. The ASPCA Animal Poison Control Center remains an Allied Agency of the University of Illinois. Several staff hold university appointments, and the center provides clinical toxicology training to veterinary toxicology residents at the College of Veterinary Medicine.

Throughout the years the center has continued to improve upon its services. In order to help the center's licensed veterinary staff more efficiently provide lifesaving information over the telephone, in November 2001, AnTox™, a unique electronic veterinary toxicology database containing more than 700,000 cases of animal poisoning, was launched. The online, direct-entry, medical-records system raises the bar by being more comprehensive and collecting more patient data than any other veterinary toxicology medical-record system in the world.

AnTox consists of two main databases that are highly integrated: the medical records database and the medical library database. This provides center staff with access to animal, clinical, substance, and therapy information. In addition to enabling staff to provide lifesaving advice quickly over the telephone, the information collected from the database also serves as a surveillance tool that helps protect and improve the lives of many animals. The data collected can be analyzed and interpreted by ASPCA Animal Poison Control Center veterinary toxicologists to identify "trends" of certain poisonings and identify improved methods of treatment. The information from each case has helped the APCC develop standardized protocols for treatment.

The APCC has played a prominent role in helping to track and either confirm or refute concerns about some products and their potential harmful effects on animals. The Internet has made it possible for "urban myths" to proliferate rapidly and cause panic among pet owners. One such case involved the cleaning and odor-treatment product, Febreze®. A rumor developed that Febreze was dangerous and causing illness and death among pets. The APCC veterinary toxicologists were able to examine their database to determine how many calls related to Febreze had been received. They also contacted the manufacturer, Proctor and Gamble, for additional information on the product's ingredients, and the concentrations of those ingredients. Based on this information, the APCC was able to state confidently that Febreze did not pose a risk to dogs or cats when used as directed.

Continuous monitoring of the cases and the database has led to several important discoveries. APCC veterinary toxicologists were the first to discover that raisins and grape skins are toxic to dogs, as is cocoa mulch. The veterinary toxicologists on staff at APCC frequently contribute new knowledge to the veterinary literature through peer-reviewed journal articles, book chapters, lectures, and continuing education programs. Pet owners across the country are able to find this information through regular updates at the ASPCA Web site, and through press coverage of interviews with APCC staff printed in newspapers, magazines, and broadcast on radio and television.

In 2002 the APCC created the Veterinary Lifeline Partner Program to make it easier for veterinarians and veterinary clinics to respond quickly and efficiently to animal poison control emergencies. Enrollment in the program is free and offers participating clinics special benefits, such as direct, around-the-clock access to specially trained veterinary professionals and board-certified veterinary toxicologists; incident summaries e-mailed or faxed for the patient's medical records; and quarterly biosurveillance alerts and toxicology tips provided via an e-newsletter. VLPP member practices are also able to access free, continuing education classes for their staff on toxicology and treatments. The ASPCA Animal Behavior Center has recently begun to work with the APCC and now offers behavior consultations to veterinary clinics as well, and continuing education in animal behavior to the VLPP member practices.

One of the most dramatic examples of the APCC's role in helping to protect America's companion animals came in spring 2007. Menu Foods, Inc., a Canadian company that produces pet foods for a number of well-known name brands, as well as a variety of store-branded products, began to receive complaints that foods it had produced were sickening pets who had eaten them. The company conducted palatability studies on some of its foods from February 27 until March 3, 2007. During this study, nine out of forty cats died of acute renal tubular necrosis. Shortly thereafter, veterinarians working for Iams pet food company received calls about renal failure in cats who had eaten a "cuts and gravy" product manufactured for Iams by Menu Foods. Iams contacted Menu Foods about the problem, and plans were put in place to begin a recall of pet foods produced by Menu Foods.

Menu Foods informed the Food and Drug Administration (FDA) about the planned recall on March 15. The recall began on March 16 and included over 60 million packages of cuts and gravy–type foods produced for more than 100 brands of pet food. Still unknown at this time was the nature of the contaminant, and how it was acting to sicken and kill both dogs and cats. Call volume at the APCC began to increase as concerned pet owners contacted the ASPCA for information on how to help their sick pets.

On March 23 the New York State Department of Agriculture announced that it had identified aminopterin, sometimes used to kill rodents, in samples of recalled foods as the substance causing the illnesses in pets. APCC veterinarians researched what was known about aminopterin and evaluated the symptoms described for cases they had handled from March 16 until March 26. They also consulted with veterinary staff at Bergh Memorial Animal Hospital, where they were treating pets who became ill after eating one of the foods identified in the recall. They found none of the clinical signs expected from poisoning by aminopterin, which include severe gastrointestinal damage and bone marrow suppression. Instead, the primary problem found in pets who had eaten the contaminated foods was renal failure, which was inconsistent with exposure to aminopterin. On March 27, the ASPCA released a statement questioning the claim that aminopterin was the cause of the problem, and called on authorities and agencies to continue their search for a contaminant that would cause symptoms consistent with those observed in the cases they had handled through the call center, and the clinical cases that were treated at Bergh Hospital.

On March 30, the APCC's doubts were confirmed when the FDA announced that they had found melamine in pet food samples. Melamine was known to be moderately toxic, and would produce urine crystals. Melamine is an industrial chemical used to manufacture plastics, and as a fertilizer. How it got into the food, and caused such significant illness, was still unknown.

Additional sleuthing eventually led investigators to China. Menu Foods had purchased wheat gluten from Chinese suppliers. Wheat gluten is added to pet foods (and human foods) to increase the protein content and to help thicken the final product. The quality of wheat gluten is based on its protein content. Protein content in something like wheat gluten is measured indirectly by measuring nitrogen levels. Melamine had been added to lower-quality wheat gluten and wheat flour to enhance their nitrogen profile and increase their monetary value.

One final discovery helped to close the loop on the mechanism by which pets were harmed. Melamine on its own would not have had the dramatic impact on pet health observed during this crisis. Eventually, it was found that in addition to melamine, cyanuric acid had been added to the wheat gluten to further enhance its nitrogen profile. While both melamine and cyanuric acid are moderately toxic, in combination, when consumed by pets, they had a devastating effect. Once consumed and absorbed into the blood, the two chemicals combined in the kidneys to produce crystals. These crystals plugged the kidney tubules, reducing and then blocking kidney function.

During the crisis the ASPCA created a Pet Food Recall Center on its Web site and provided regular updates to the public and animal health professionals on what was known, how to treat affected pets, and even provided links to information on how to make nutritionally balanced homemade pet food. The APCC and the ASPCA quickly became the go-to place for accurate, unbiased information on the pet food recall.

Senior veterinary staff from the APCC and Bergh Hospital were regulars on the nightly news, and frequently quoted in print coverage on the recall. From March 18 until April 2, 2007, more than 500 news stories were generated on the topic, with content provided by the ASPCA. This resulted in some 300 million impressions, and placed the ASPCA as the most frequently consulted authority during the crisis. Senator Richard Durbin from Illinois called hearings on the federal government's response to the crisis and its failure to prevent it. As of April 2007, the FDA Web site confirmed sixteen deaths directly related to the contaminated products, although the agency acknowledged receiving roughly seventeen thousand consumer complaints. Most knowledgeable sources estimate that deaths, although not confirmed, numbered in the thousands. Additional hearings and new legislation are expected. ASPCA experts will likely continue to play a role as this process goes on.

Henry Bergh portrait. This portrait of Henry Bergh, painted by John Wood Dodge, hangs in the ASPCA boardroom.
All photos courtesy ASPCA Archives.

ASPCA Seal. The ASPCA seal was designed by publisher and illustrator Frank Leslie. It depicts a fallen cart horse, a teamster beating the horse, and an avenging angel rising up to protect the horse. Versions of this seal are used by ASPCAs across the country.

Horse ambulance. Henry Bergh invented the horse ambulance and introduced it to the streets of New York in 1867. The slings, slides, and derricks that Bergh developed are still used in animal rescue work today.

Puck finds Bergh "The Only Mourner" to follow the dog cart to the New York pound

Bergh and pound animals. In this cartoon from *Puck*, Henry Bergh is lampooned for his sentimental concern for the stray animals of New York City.

Kit Burns. Kit Burns was a well-known impresario of animal fighting and engaged in a cat and mouse game with Henry Bergh and the ASPCA until his arrest by New York City police.

Horse bathing. Among the free services that the ASPCA offered for working horses were free baths at their ambulance houses.

Veterinary care for horses. The first hospital the ASPCA opened, in 1912, was for horses. An ingenious series of overhead tracks and tilting tables facilitated the care and treatment of injured horses.

Children marching for kindness. In the 1920s Young Defender groups were formed in New York City public schools, and children would march under a humane education banner during parades.

Girl Scouts. The ASPCA headquarters at the corner of East 92nd Street and York Avenue included a classroom with a small menagerie. School groups and scouts were invited to visit and learn about animals and their care.

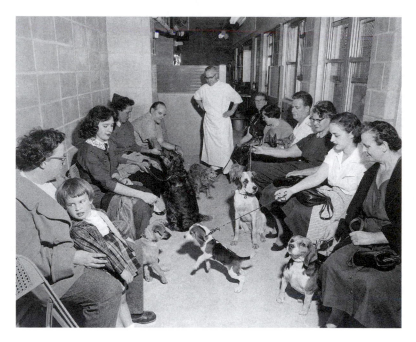

Hospital waiting room. During the Great Depression, 70 percent of the clients at the ASPCA animal hospital were charity cases.

Field staff. When the ASPCA took over animal control duties for the City of New York in 1894, they hired and trained a salaried staff to ensure proper care and treatment of animals. This group of field staff are attired in jaunty jodhpurs and riding boots.

A.S.P.C.A.
HOLDING PENS

To Eliminate Shackling and Hoisting of Live, Conscious Slaughterhouse Animals

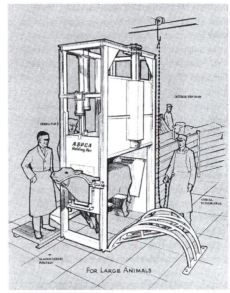

For Large Animals

Above: The ASPCA Holding Pen for large animals—steers, cows, and bulls. Its use has been approved by rabbinical leaders with jurisdiction over ritualistic slaughter. It meets all requirements of the Meat Inspection Division of the U.S. Department of Agriculture. Two such pens are now in operation and two more are available to meat packers through the ASPCA.

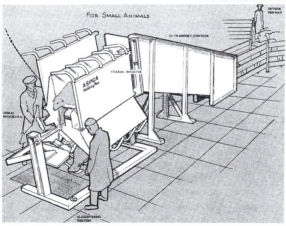

The ASPCA Holding Pen designed for small animals—sheep, calves, and lambs. Drawings and specifications for this Pen are in the hands of ASPCA patent attorneys. A prototype will be built promptly and tested under slaughterhouse conditions to demonstrate humane handling of small animals and economy and safety for packers.

Slaughter pens. The ASPCA acquired two patents to pens for the humane slaughter of livestock, and made the plans available to meatpackers for no charge. Versions of these pens are still in use today.

Dog license sales. Actress Joan Blondell and her pet pug help to promote dog license sales in 1958. At its peak, the ASPCA licensed over 250,000 dogs a year in New York City.

Animalport. The ASPCA Animalport at JFK airport provided a variety of services for animals in transit.

Animal Precinct. Today's Bergh's men (and women) are featured on the Animal Planet television show, *Animal Precinct*.

Rescue in New Orleans. In the weeks following Hurricane Katrina, ASPCA staff deployed to New Orleans to assist with animal rescue operations.

Big Fix Rig. As part of the Hurricanes Katrina and Rita recovery efforts in the Gulf Coast region of the United States, the ASPCA and other groups have provided funding for the Big Fix Rig, a mobile spay and neuter clinic that reaches areas with limited veterinary services.

ASPCA adoption van. The ASPCA mobile adoption van travels to events and neighborhoods in New York City to promote the adoption of shelter pets.

ASPCA cat habitat. Renovations at the ASPCA shelter have eliminated cages in the adoption area. Cats are provided with an open environment that allows more room for exercise and social behavior.

ASPCA Day. ASPCA President Ed Sayres addresses an enthusiastic crowd at the ASPCA Day celebration in New York's Union Square on April 10, 2007.

Chapter 7

Training and Behavior

I n 1944 the ASPCA's Education department enlisted pioneering dog-obedience instructor Blanche Saunders to conduct a ten-week obedience course for the public. Promotional materials at that time pointed out, "Dogs and owners are always trained together, the theory being that we teach *you* to train your dog," and further emphasized, "bad-mannered dogs are a hazard in traffic, an annoyance to neighbors and a nuisance to landlords." This was certainly an early affirmation of the importance of training, and suggested that training programs can help strengthen the relationship between persons, pets, and the public. This philosophy continues to inform and guide the society's activities.

Americans in large numbers were introduced to the idea of trained dogs through the exploits of film stars such as Strongheart and Rin-Tin-Tin, Lassie, Buck in *Call of the Wild*, and Toto in *The Wizard of Oz*, among many lesser-known names from the twenties and thirties. Strongheart was trained in Germany as a police dog, and Rin-Tin-Tin was brought to America as a puppy after World War I by serviceman Corporal Lee Duncan, who found him in a largely destroyed kennel of German "war dogs." Americans had long used dogs for hunting and working on farms, so dog training was not completely novel. But while these practical working dogs certainly needed to be trained to be attentive to their owners and to understand what *not* to do, their primary work consisted of following the instincts that had been bred into them, whether to herd and protect livestock, trail game, or point and retrieve game birds. Obedience, on the other hand, involved training a dog to do a human handler's bidding in a setting that offered no natural cues. The exercises simulated the tasks that a field dog might be expected to perform, such as waiting at his handler's side until sent to retrieve, or coming when called to sit in front of his handler to "deliver to hand"—but all without an actual bird as an inducement!

The idea that ordinary dog owners could teach their pets to respond to a series of commands, such as "sit," "come," and "stay" was first popularized in the early 1930s, when Mrs. Helene Whitehouse Walker, the wealthy owner and breeder of standard poodles imported from England, began to resent the fact that her friends disparaged the intelligence of her "sissy" dogs. Walker was aware that under American Kennel Club (AKC) rules, poodles were not eligible to compete in AKC-licensed field trials—events that tested a hunting dog's ability to perform the specific tasks that his breed was originally developed to carry out. So Walker set out to find another way to prove that her poodles were as smart as any pointer, setter, or retriever.

Walker had read about obedience tests in English dog magazines. The tests were sponsored by the Associated Sheep, Police, and Army Dog Society, which was formed in 1924 to test working dogs but had recently opened its events to include all breeds. Walker traveled to England and spent six weeks observing the tests and learning how to train her own dogs to perform the exercises. What was unique about the new "obedience" was that the dog's owner was taught how to train and compete with her own dog. Previously, and contemporaneously as well, whatever training was done was carried out by breeders of working and sporting dogs, or by experts (often the same people) who "started" a dog's training for a fee. Training had never before been conceived of as something that the average dog owner, especially an urban or suburban dog owner, might accomplish.

Upon her return to America, Walker began a one-woman crusade to persuade the American Kennel Club to sanction what she called "obedience test field trials," a new sport in which all breeds would be eligible to compete for points toward titles. She held training classes at her home, wrote a book of procedures for handlers, judges, and clubs, convinced local dog clubs to offer competitions in connection with their annual dog shows, and wrote letters to newspapers inviting reporters to attend the tests in order to cover the new sport. Then, in the fall of 1934, Walker advertised for kennel help, and Blanche Saunders, a farm girl from Brewster, New York, answered the ad. Saunders showed so much aptitude with the dogs that Walker taught her all she knew about training, and in no time at all, Saunders was doing the training.

By 1937, there was a fair amount of sustained interest and activity in obedience in New York and the Northeast, but Mrs. Walker knew that in order for dog training to gain widespread acceptance, the rest of the country had to become engaged. That year she and Blanche Saunders hooked a twenty-one-foot trailer to a 1935 Buick sedan, and with three standard poodles, set out on a cross-country road trip. As unusual as it was for two women to travel alone in 1937, the duo covered 10,000 miles in ten weeks, giving obedience exhibitions at dog shows and other venues in the Midwest, Southwest, and Far West. During the years of World War II, Mrs. Walker first reduced her breeding activity and then closed her kennel, leaving the kennel name and several brood bitches to her protégé, Blanche Saunders.

From the late thirties until the midfifties, Saunders orchestrated obedience demonstrations at locations as diverse as the Westminster Kennel Club dog show; in Yankee Stadium, with 50,000 baseball fans in attendance; and in front of lunchtime crowds at Rockefeller Center during National Dog Week—an event that began in 1928 and received funding from the Gaines Dog Research Center and later from the Pet Food Institute and others. From the beginning, obedience training was presented as an activity well within the capability of the ordinary owner and the ordinary dog. Its purpose was to make the dog a more agreeable companion in the home, in public, and in the presence of other dogs.

When the United States entered World War II, Saunders began to work with Josef Weber, a former military dog trainer who had emigrated from Germany after World War I. England, France, Belgium, and other nations in Europe had used dogs in their military operations during World War I, although none as systematically as Germany. Saunders assisted Weber in training dogs in basic obedience for the United States War Dog Program, popularly called the "K-9 Corps." World War II was the first time that the United States used dogs in earnest for military operations, and the government was dependent on private trainers both to procure the dogs and to train them. Patriotic dog breeders and fanciers as well as ordinary pet owners responded to the call for dogs for the War Dog Program. At first thirty different breeds were accepted, but experience soon narrowed the list to five: German shepherd dogs, Belgian sheepdogs, Doberman pinschers, giant schnauzers, and farm collies. Crosses of these breeds were also accepted. Roughly 20,000 dogs were procured by the U.S. military during the Second World War, although only half that number actually completed training or served in the field (the other half failed to meet the requirements for a variety of reasons). When the war was over, the donated dogs were "rehabilitated" and returned to their civilian owners, often with great fanfare. Some were given medals and citations for bravery, and one, Chips, even received the Purple Heart for being wounded in action. These accolades were later revoked amid complaints that the citations were cheapened by being bestowed upon a dog.

Beginning in 1946 and continuing to the present time, the military began to purchase dogs outright from proven sources (currently only German shepherds and Belgian Malinois are used). After World War II, the dogs were no longer returned to civilian homes after service, primarily because of liability issues. This was not widely known, however, and when Americans found out well after the fact that roughly 3,500 of the 4,000 military dogs who served in Vietnam were either euthanized or given to the South Vietnamese Army when U.S. troops pulled out, the public was outraged. In 2000, Representative Roscoe Bartlett of Maryland learned of a particular Belgian Malinois named Robby who was no longer able to work, but because of current government policy, could not be adopted by his handler. Realizing that Robby would be euthanized, Bartlett introduced legislation that would allow military working dogs who were no longer of use to the armed forces to be "retired," after which they could be adopted by their handlers or by law enforcement agencies. Senator Bob Smith of New Hampshire sponsored the Senate version of the bill. The ASPCA national office in Washington, D.C., lobbied for the "Robby Bill," and ASPCA members in large numbers contacted their legislators to ask them to vote "yes." The bill passed both houses, and President Clinton signed it into law in November 2000. Unfortunately, Robby's handler could not afford the medical care that the aging canine would require, so the adoption never took place. Robby spent his last months on a military base and was euthanized in January 2001. He was buried at Hartsdale Pet Cemetery, the nation's first and most prestigious burial ground for pets, in a moving ceremony that was well attended by supporters of the "Robby Bill."

Between all the publicity about the War Dog Program and the new anyone-can-do-it method of dog training, New York City dog owners were primed to respond favorably to a short item in the *New York Times* on July 5, 1944, with the headline, "Course for Dogs Set: ASPCA Announces 10-Week Class to Improve Canine Manners." There was already a tremendous amount of interest in the concept, and a more qualified instructor than Blanche Saunders could scarcely be found anywhere. Saunders taught obedience classes at the ASPCA for the next seventeen years. It is estimated that roughly 17,000 dogs participated in the program during that time. Not coincidentally, the poodle's popularity soared during the same time frame. It was in the years following World War II that purebred dogs became a status symbol with millions of ordinary Americans, reversing the widespread earlier view that purebreds were unhealthy and high-strung compared to so-called mutts.

Saunders wrote several books on obedience training that went through many printings and editions by different publishers. Her 1946 book and film by the name of *Training You to Train Your Dog*—the film was narrated by actress Helen Hayes and broadcaster Lowell Thomas—were among the earliest in the "how-to" genre of dog training materials that today easily number in the many hundreds, if not thousands. Because Saunders had learned her craft under individuals whose background was in training dogs for the military, her methods were a little heavy-handed by today's standards. The technique was primarily one of well-timed praise and reward for correct responses, but collar corrections and verbal reprimands were also employed. It was one-size-fits-all training, for dogs large and small, bold and timid. Short training sessions, repetition, and consistency were stressed. Coursework included training pets to walk at heel, sit, stay, come, lie down, and stop barking—on command.

Blanche Saunders's training classes under the ASPCA's sponsorship were marketed to the public. The ASPCA's shelters in all five boroughs were filled with thousands of stray, abandoned, and relinquished dogs who would be held the mandatory length of time and then destroyed. At that time there was no thought of training these dogs in order to improve their chances for adoption. That concept was many years in the future, not only at the ASPCA, but everywhere. The strain on the society's staff, space, and finances of managing the sheer volume of animals in New York City precluded any effort to do more than literally feed and shelter the unwanted dogs and cats before euthanizing them to make room for more.

But change was in the air. The field of dog training was anything but static in the second half of the twentieth century. On one hand, the various formal dog sports (obedience, field trials, and so-called "working dog" sports, such as German-inspired Schutzhund trials) became more and more competitive, leading many handlers and professional trainers to enhance their dogs' performance by using punishment along with praise and other positive methods of reinforcing behavior. Some professionals who made their living training other people's dogs had to achieve results much faster than could be accomplished with the average dog in brief training sessions using only praise and petting. But other handlers and trainers went in the opposite direction. As they accumulated experience from working with many different breeds and types of dogs, young and old, they began to realize that all dogs had an innate temperament that made them more or less easy to train. They recognized that what was needed was deeper understanding of canine behavior, and especially of how dogs learn. At first, it was tempting to generalize: golden retrievers were outgoing and eager to please, and therefore easy to train. Terriers were feisty and quarrelsome and stubborn, and therefore hard to train.

Then, in 1965, a soon-to-be classic text, *Genetics and the Social Behavior of Dogs*, by J. P. Scott and J. L. Fuller, was published. Based on thirteen years of research with five breeds of dogs representing the major dog groups, the book established that not only was there a genetic component to behavior (supporting breed-based characteristics), but also that the experiences that a puppy had in early life, good and bad, could affect the animal's future behavior. What this meant to trainers was that one method really might not suit all. It also suggested that behavior could be changed through training. None of this came quickly, easily, or in a linear fashion. But as more and more dogs moved indoors full-time, more and more families, often with no one at home during the day, needed a dog with good indoor behavior. Suddenly everyone was talking about training a dog not to chew the furniture, or not to bark when left at home alone. Trainers and do-it-yourselfers alike began comparing notes and sharing tips. The thirst for information was insatiable. Articles, books, columns, videotapes, clinics, seminars, workshops, and conferences sprang up to meet the need.

When John F. Kullberg, Ed.D., became the society's chief executive officer in 1978, he brought to the position a conviction that ethology—the study of the way animals behave in their natural environment—was critical to understanding animals' needs and providing for their welfare. Even as he wrestled with the ASPCA's growing financial problems and the public's generally negative assessment of the society's performance, Kullberg began to recruit individuals with academic backgrounds and training in relevant sciences. He first hired Ann Squire, Ph.D., whose doctorate was in animal behavior, to head the Education department. Squire contributed insight on animal behavior to the society's education programs and other ASPCA activities, including legislation and advocacy. In turn, her choice to run the society's dog training program, which had always been a function of the Education department, was Micky Niego, an individual with a degree in industrial psychology—a discipline involved with motivation in a work environment. Historically the ASPCA had supported continuing education for staff members, and the burgeoning national interest in all things canine provided ample opportunities to learn. Squire encouraged Niego to attend as many conferences as she could to learn and stay abreast of developments in the field of training and behavior, and in time to present workshops of her own on evaluating and training shelter dogs. By 1984, Niego had set up a new department called Companion Animal Services (CAS), and the next year rolled out a Companion Animal Behavior Counseling Helpline. This innovative, free service was extremely popular with people who had adopted a dog or cat from the ASPCA shelter and needed advice with common behavior problems once they got their new pet home. The helpline soon was extended to the general public. It was one of the ASPCA's first focused efforts at keeping adopted pets in their new homes, and went a long way in countering the perception that the society did nothing but kill animals. Currently the ASPCA is working to develop a national Web-based "lifeline" service for pets with behavior problems.

The Education department at this point in time was situated in a rabbit warren of small cubicles in the building's basement, isolated from the flow of traffic into and out of the shelter and hospital. This allowed staff to bring a dog or two into the department to spend time, and accidentally favored the evolution of several new ASPCA programs. The Delta Society, founded in Washington State in 1977 to explore the positive effects of animals on human health, had already held several national conferences on what was rapidly becoming the catchphrase of the day: the "human-animal bond" (HAB). Niego attended the first Delta Society conference in 1986 and many thereafter. These conferences engendered a tremendous amount of interest in what loosely was being called "pet therapy." Individuals in training classes and dog clubs were encouraged to participate in informal programs of visiting nursing homes and other institutions with their pets in order to bring a few hours of pleasure to residents. In the first rush of enthusiasm to share in this rewarding experience, few if any precautions were taken. Beginning in 1987, Companion Animal Services staff from the ASPCA took dogs from the shelter on these visits, at first without even the benefit of a bath. In retrospect, they marvel that there were no serious negative consequences. Sometimes, Niego took her bullmastiff, Jake, on visits. Jake was a well-socialized and outgoing dog who was allowed to roam the ASPCA building on his own in search of friends who gave him treats. Most often, however, it was the shelter dogs who went on the visits.

During these outings, staff began to notice certain qualities about the dogs they took with them. Once back at the ASPCA, they wrote their observations on the dogs' cage cards. Observations included such things as "very friendly/accepts all people," "good lap dog/does not struggle," "allows grooming and nail-clipping," and "takes treat well/good around food." Before long, they noticed that the dogs with notations on their cards were getting adopted more readily. In particular, older, plain brown or black dogs who just didn't stand out in the shelter population, were getting homes. The comments on their cards seemed to bring them to life, and the adoptions staff could steer a potential adopter to a specific dog. It gave the dogs, who more often than not came into the shelter with no history, a bit of background. These "pet therapy evaluations" were the precursors to general shelter evaluations. It was the first systematic attempt to "match-make." There was no adoption application in place at this time, which meant that virtually any person could adopt any dog or cat, no questions asked. That would soon change, as well, and the society instituted an adoption contract that allowed it to refuse an animal to a specific individual if warranted. Spay/neuter within six months for all adopted animals had been compulsory since 1973, however.

In the meantime, the Delta Society, firmly focused on studying and promoting the ways in which animals benefit human health and well-being, had published its first set of guidelines for animals in nursing homes, and was in the process of funding $350,000 worth of research studies on human–animal interactions. Over the next few years, Delta fine-tuned the screening criteria for animals who would visit institutions, and developed a comprehensive training program with two tracks: one for "animal-assisted therapy" and one for "animal-assisted activities." The 8,000, all-volunteer handler-and-animal teams that are at the heart of both applications—designated in 1990 as Delta Society Pet Partners®— are found in communities all across the United States. Delta-designated "evaluators" certify the volunteers and their dogs, cats, birds, rabbits, and other pets who meet the criteria for "visiting animals." The ASPCA became a Delta Society training, evaluation, and certification partner in the early 1990s—a relationship that continues today. But in 1986, years before all of this had been ironed out, Micky Niego's bullmastiff, Jake, who hung out every day in the Education department's basement office, received the Delta Society's very first Therapy Animal of the Year Award.

In June 2007, NBC's *Today* show featured Angel on a Leash, a pet visitation program founded in 2004 as a charitable activity of the Westminster Kennel Club. The story included a segment that was filmed in the ASPCA's training center, with Delta evaluator Michelle Siegel of the Bronx, who trains and certifies Pet Partner teams who participate in such programs in the New York metropolitan area. That same week Micky Niego, who has operated her own dog behavior consulting business since leaving the ASPCA in 1993, came to the society's training center to have Siegel recertify her current bullmastiff therapy dog.

An exciting new initiative launched at the ASPCA in 2006 is the Potential Pet Partners Program. A joint effort of the ASPCA, Delta Society, and the Pet Project Alliance, a New York City–based nonprofit dedicated to fostering the human–animal bond, the program identifies shelter dogs who have the potential to become visiting therapy animals.

Those who meet the requirements have a tag placed on their kennels as well as some printed materials about the Pet Partners program. Being designated a potential pet partner also helps the dog find a new home.

As soon as the Companion Animal Services staff in the mid-1980s saw the benefit that being out of the kennels had on the shelter dogs, the department stumbled on the idea of "office fostering" to improve behavior and enhance adoptability. They began to bring dogs from the shelter into their department to spend the day, along with their personal pets from home, and shelter dogs that they were fostering at home. The director fostered cats in her office.

The physical space itself had a serendipitous effect. There was a small kitchen area with a refrigerator and microwave. Staff ate together at a long table in the classroom, which also contained a sofa and chairs. They snacked at their desks and threw scraps into their wastebaskets. In the library, there were shelves of books and a few old leather chairs. There was a coat tree and umbrella stand. It was homey. Thus, the natural behaviors of the numerous dogs loose in the space at the same time held full sway. They scavenged for food in the wastebaskets. They lifted their legs on the coat tree and umbrella stand. They chewed on bookshelves. As they did so, the training staff was able to correct these natural behaviors that nevertheless would not be appreciated in a new home. The environment was a learning laboratory for both animals and people. Not only did it allow staff to develop reliable information about dogs for adoption, but it gave one staff member, Sue Sternberg, the idea for a "real life room," modeled on the homelike setting in the Education department at that time. Sternberg went on to develop this concept as a tool that shelters could utilize to give their dogs a break from the noise and stress of life in a concrete kennel. Today, many of the country's most modern shelters include variations on Sternberg's "real life room" to house animals and display them to the public.

Another function of the Education department was to produce a variety of publications for the society, including the *ASPCA Quarterly Report* and its successor, *ASPCA Animal Watch* magazine, which also came out four times a year. ASPCA staff from various departments were recruited to contribute columns in their area of expertise for each issue. Beginning in 1986, Micky Niego covered training and behavior in a column called Companion Lines. Jacque Lynn Schultz, Niego's successor as director of Companion Animal Services, inherited the column in 1993 and wrote quarterly installments for more than ten years, until *Animal Watch* was discontinued in 2004. Subsequently all of the Companion Lines articles were reprinted and are sold inexpensively as packets, one for cats and one for dogs, designed to be copied and distributed at shelters. Each packet includes twenty-two different behavior problem-solving articles in three easy-to-use formats: booklet, master copies, and on CD.

As Companion Animal Services grew, other significant initiatives were put in place. For the better part of fifty years, the ASPCA was one of the very few places in Manhattan with enough space to be able to hold classes where a dog owner could take her pet for group training with other dogs and handlers—the precise scenario that New York City dog owners confront on a daily basis. Not to say that the training space was ideal. In what today's longtime staff members refer to as the "old" building, on Ninety-second Street and York Avenue, classes were taught in the parking lot if weather permitted. Other times they were taught in the garage where the humane law enforcement vehicles were otherwise parked. In the new headquarters, half a block to the west, it was worse. According to Jacque Lynn Schultz, a certified pet dog trainer who taught at both locations, the subcellar garage in the new facility had poor lighting and "no HVAC." Heat lamps were mounted on the walls to provide a little warmth in the winter. "You baked if you were directly underneath them, and froze if you were more than six feet away," Schultz recalls. "The conditions were awful, but the students were loyal, and we had a thriving program running three nights a week and Saturdays." By 2000, major renovations in the building had been completed, and a brand-new behavior clinic and training center opened on the second floor, complete with low-impact flooring and acoustical tiles on the ceiling.

In 1988 John Kullberg hired Stephen Zawistowski, Ph.D., a scientist and certified applied-animal behaviorist, to head up the Education department and continue the development of the animal behavior and training programs. Zawistowski was also charged with revitalizing the ASPCA's standing as a national organization. Nearly a century of running animal control for the city of New York had obscured the society's visibility outside the city.

Because Helene Whitehouse Walker was involved with competitive obedience, obedience training classes modeled on her original set of exercises were often out of sync with the needs of the average pet owner, who would never see the inside of a competition ring and could care less if her family pet ever walked precisely at heel on her left side, neither forging a few inches ahead nor lagging a few inches behind. Still, it was not until the 1980s that a more sensible training program evolved that truly had the ordinary owner and ordinary dog in mind. This was the Canine Good Citizen program.

Jacque Lynn Schultz taught basic obedience classes for the ASPCA, but also offered other programs in keeping with the public's evolving interests. She extended the ASPCA's training classes to Saturdays, and when the AKC came out with its Canine Good Citizen (CGC) program in 1989, Schultz was one of the first trainers in New York to prepare owners and dogs to be tested for this new certificate. CGC was the AKC's very first program that was open to unregistered and mixed-breed dogs as well as to purebreds. The Canine Good Citizen test is noncompetive. It evaluates a dog's ability to remain under reasonable control of his owner in everyday situations involving strangers and other dogs. The AKC estimates that 500,000 dogs have been awarded the CGC certificate to date. Therapy Dogs International, the United States' oldest organization to register dogs to visit patients in hospitals and other settings, requires a dog to pass the CGC test in order to be certified, and the Delta Society has adopted the CGC test as a major part of the "skills" portion of its certification process for dogs. In the mid-1990s Schultz developed a "Fun 'n' Games" class, which combined agility (a new steeplechase for dogs, imported from England in the 1980s), musical freestyle ("dancing with dogs"), and tricks training. The Fun 'n' Games class was a great favorite of those wishing to continue training beyond earning their CGC certificates.

The ASPCA was up to a lot more than fun and games, however. Starting in the 1990s, Zawistowski and his staff began to conduct research projects related to animal behavior, the human–animal bond, and animal adoptions. Possibly the first formal, shelter-based behavior evaluations attempted in the United States, the data resulted in an informal "poster presentation" at the Animal Behavior Society (ABS) meetings on methods for the evaluation of behavior of shelter dogs, distribution of problems presented to the behavior helpline, and resources used by dog owners seeking behavior and training information. A separate study about companion-animal response to the loss of an animal companion, based on observations by pet owners of surviving pets in multiple-pet homes, was presented at the International Conference on Human-Animal Interactions in Geneva, in 1995. During this time, staff also participated in the development and review process of more than fifteen ASPCA books on pet care and training.

As the field of applied animal behavior developed in terms of companion-animal programs during the 1990s, it became clear that some divisions were appearing among three main groups—dog trainers, applied behaviorists, and veterinarians. In 1991, the Animal Behavior Society, a nonprofit scientific society founded to study animal behavior, initiated a certification program for academically trained behaviorists with applied experience. The ASPCA's Stephen Zawistowski chaired the ABS's Board of Professional Certification from 1998 until 2007. The American College of Veterinary Behaviorists was formed later in the 1990s. The three complementary fields of dog trainers, animal behaviorists, and veterinarians did not always work in a cooperative fashion. A distinct effort was made by the ASPCA to bring these fields together in order to promote the human–animal bond, support adoptions, and provide pet owners with appropriate behavioral interventions. Amy Marder, V.M.D., joined the ASPCA in 1999 as vice president of Behavioral Medicine and Companion Animal Services until 2001, when Pamela Reid, Ph.D., certified applied animal behaviorist, took over.

It was during the tenure of Dr. Marder that the ASPCA opened its Center for Behavioral Therapy, housed in the headquarters building in Manhattan. This event punctuated the growth of programs in animal behavior at the ASPCA. Dr. Marder initiated a program of training and socializing the society's shelter dogs and cats to enhance their adoptability. Micky Niego had begun what she called "diagnostic dog walking" for the society's shelter dogs in 1988. Marder went a step further by eliciting staff and volunteers to bring shelter dogs to the training center on their lunch hours. Interested staff members who had gone through a mandated initiation process to become "dog walkers" selected dogs from the kennels to spend an hour walking in the neighborhood, going to the nearby park, and doing some basic obedience and agility work in the training center. In the initiation training, the dog walkers learned how to put a head halter on the dog, attach a leash, and safely bring him or her out of the kennel. Marder ended each session by having staff sit on the floor and gently massage the dogs, teaching them to relax and enjoy the kind of physical handling that a new adoptive family might employ. Everything was geared toward acclimating the dog to what he or she might encounter in a new home. The fact that these sessions were conducted in a group setting accustomed the shelter dogs to associating good times with the presence of other dogs and other people, always an important consideration in a congested urban environment like New York City.

In addition to evaluating dogs and cats when they first came in to the shelter, and to designing behavior modification programs to correct any problems the animals demonstrated, Dr. Marder also did private consultations with city residents whose pets had "issues." She worked with problem behaviors that ranged from cats who had stopped using their litter boxes to dogs who were mutilating themselves, destroying their owners' furnishings, or howling nonstop when left alone. As one of the then-small fraternity of veterinary behaviorists in the country, Dr. Marder was a pioneer in prescribing pharmacological agents in conjunction with behavior modification and other therapies to resolve problems. As a veterinarian, she always looked first for medical causes when a dog or cat exhibited abnormal behavior. And like many other ASPCA department heads, Dr. Marder began writing a regular column for *Animal Watch* magazine, in which she discussed some of her interesting cases.

During her time with the ASPCA, Dr. Marder developed an exhaustive assessment tool for the purpose of trying to learn whether the way a dog responded on a behavior evaluation test in the shelter was predictive of how that animal would behave once placed in a new home. Called the MATCH-UP (Marder Animal Rescue League Test for Canine Homing using Understanding and Predictability), the data collected over a two-year period with ASPCA shelter dogs created some important new knowledge for the field.

The staff of the Center for Behavioral Therapy began to work closely with the society's Humane Law Enforcement (HLE) department, providing behavioral evaluations of animals from cruelty cases and long-term enrichment and rehabilitation programs for them. Animals seized as part of a cruelty case must often spend extended periods of time in medical treatment and then in the shelter until the courts complete the prosecution of the cruelty charges. When *Animal Precinct*, the reality program featuring the ASPCA's HLE officers, debuted on Animal Planet in 2001, the center staff often found themselves in front of the camera as they performed their evaluations and made recommendations.

When Pamela J. Reid, Ph.D., succeeded Dr. Marder as the head of the society's training and behavior programs, the Center for Behavioral Therapy became the Animal Behavior Center under her direction, reflecting Reid's different academic background as a certified applied animal behaviorist. Beginning in 2002, Reid and Zawistowski, now the executive vice-president of ASPCA National Programs, instituted an animal behavior fellowship program for recent Ph.D. graduates in animal behavior. Successful applicants are granted a two-year fellowship at the Animal Behavior Center—which relocated in 2005 to the ASPCA's Midwest office in Urbana, Illinois—during which they prepare for a career in applied animal behavior. The program is designed to provide the fellows with the skills and experience required to achieve certification through the ABS's Board of Professional Certification. Three behavior fellows have graduated to date and are practicing clinical animal behavior in California, Arizona, and New York.

The ASPCA is also helping to produce new professionals in the behavior field by collaborating with the biology department at the University of Illinois to offer a master of science degree in applied animal behavior. The new program was launched in fall 2006.

In its new home in Illinois, the Animal Behavior Center also offers continuing education for animal trainers, veterinarians, and other professionals, as well as pet behavior research for the scientific community, and in-home consultations for local area pet owners. The center plans to roll out a national Web-based behavior lifeline service for owners of pets with behavior problems. Reid and her associates disseminate up-to-date information on companion animal behavior through seminars, speaking engagements, and publications.

The ASPCA Animal Behavior Center provides legal services, as well. Staff evaluate dogs to determine if they're "dangerous" and provide expert witness testimony in cases involving companion animals. Dr. Reid's 1996 book, *Excel-Erated Learning: Explaining in Plain English How Dogs Learn and How Best to Teach Them*, does just as the title promises.

Chapter 8

Enforcing the Law

A s soon as Henry Bergh had his charter and a new anticruelty law in his pocket, he started to enforce it on the streets of New York. Although a gentleman from his top hat to his toes, Bergh was fearless, tenacious, and inexhaustible in pursuit of justice for animals who were being caused to suffer. He began the work alone, although he never hesitated to call upon the city police to assist him, as indeed the law required them to do. As word of his mission and success grew, more and more citizens contacted him to report cruelty, and he began to hire staff to work as agents of the society. In the society's early days, these agents were known far and wide as "Bergh's men."

Although he joined the staff too late to be called a Bergh's man, William Michael Ryan, who was hired in 1912, was the archetype of the ASPCA special agent for most of the society's history. In the early days of ASPCA law enforcement, the society depended on men (and *men* they were) who came to the organization with some experience working with animals. Bill Ryan was a typical example. His father had been a horseman, and Ryan had substantial experience with this most common target of the ASPCA's cruelty investigations at the time when he joined the organization. One of Ryan's heralded rescues involved a fire in a horse stable. Then, as now, horses were housed on the second and even third floors of wooden structures, with the carriages and other conveyances that the horses pulled parked on the street level as a matter of convenience. A fire had broken out on the stable's lower level, and the ASPCA was summoned. Unable to lead the horses down and out of the building, Ryan risked personal injury by going up into the stable. Upon noticing that open windows of the stable aligned with windows of an adjacent building, he got the idea of fashioning a bridge between the buildings out of wooden planks. Then, using empty feed sacks to cover the horses' heads in order to calm them, Ryan led them across the makeshift bridge to safety.

In addition to experience with animals, agents typically were men with ingenuity, a sense of adventure, and loads of patience. They often combined the skills of horse doctor, cowboy, social worker, and cop. In many situations, the "cop" part was the last of the roles they would play.

Agents worked in New York City. This meant they dealt with people from a wide variety of cultures. They often needed to explain that animals were not treated cruelly in America, and that there was a law against such cruelty. While Ryan was the best known of his generation, he was not alone in his dedication to the job and flair for the dramatic.

In the late 1960s and 1970s, an ex-rodeo clown agent named Tommy "Cowboy" Langdon amazed his colleagues and others with his ability to anticipate an animal's behavior and easily capture it, often with little more than a rope with a loop in it. One of his most extraordinary exploits involved a house fire. The family, huddled on the street, begged someone to save their two dogs, still in the building. When one of the dogs was heard howling, Cowboy leapt into action. He tossed his rope over his shoulder and raced into the building. He seemed to be gone for far too long when he reappeared at a third-floor window with a dog under each arm. Flames blocked his retreat back down the stairs, and before firemen could bring a ladder into position, the roaring fire was licking at his back. Cowboy tightened his grip on both dogs and leapt from the window. Witnesses at the scene recall the sound of bones snapping as he struck the pavement and rolled to protect the dogs. Both legs were broken, and Cowboy was laid up for a bit, but once healed, he was back on the street with rope in hand—maybe more bowlegged than before.

Eventually the respect afforded to ASPCA agents would erode. Issues that drove changes within the New York City Police Department (NYPD) had the same effect on ASPCA agents. For instance, baby boomers will remember that this was the era when it was common not only to question authority, but to challenge it as well. The sixties had happened, with all its antiauthority excesses. Police officers were no longer kind fellows who walked a regular beat, checking locks on business doors, and asking folks they hadn't seen before in the neighborhood if they were "lost." The days of a kindly Bill Ryan pitching a bit of blarney to resolve a dispute were receding into a gauzy past. Organizers and spectators in dogfights and cockfights were often members of violent street gangs. Along with the dogs and cocks seized in raids, agents would now collect assault weapons and drugs.

Most ironic was the criticism that the ASPCA routinely received for its failure to end animal cruelty by simply arresting the people who were mistreating the animals. As the burgeoning animal rights movement began to influence the way people thought about animals, the agents were still enforcing nineteenth century laws. Raising veal calves in small crates was cruel. Breeding dogs in puppy mills was cruel. Conducting experiments on animals was cruel. If all these actions were cruel, why couldn't the society formed for the prevention of cruelty to animals use its law-enforcement authority to end these practices?

The answer was that many of the anticruelty laws, now a century old, either exempted certain practices or simply did not address them. The court system, never well versed in this area of law, was overwhelmed by the number of other cases brought before it. Crime rates were exploding in the 1970s and 1980s. Violent crimes, drug crimes, and cases driven by civil disobedience bloated the dockets. There were "real" crimes to try and punish—and dogs, cats, and chickens were not high on the priority list.

Civil disobedience provided a special concern for the society. As the animal protection activists adopted the tactics of other social movements, the question arose again and again: Where was the ASPCA? When activists walked picket lines, where was the ASPCA? When it came time to risk arrest through civil disobedience, where was the ASPCA? It was a critical question within the organization: how to reconcile being a law enforcement agency with the desire to join other animal groups engaged in high profile actions to help animals. Would the NYPD respond to a request for help from ASPCA agents if they had arrested other ASPCA staff at a demonstration earlier in the day? In the end, the leaders at the ASPCA decided that the organization's original mission, and success, had been to be a force within the law enforcement community. The society would not jeopardize its reputation and standing with other law enforcement agencies.

Other men joined the ASPCA and worked their way up through the system. Mark MacDonald, now a thirty-year veteran and counting, came to the ASPCA after working at the New York Aquarium. He started as a kennel man in one of the shelters, and then was assigned to the ASPCA's Animalport at John F. Kennedy International Airport (then Idlewild Field). At that time, the ASPCA was managing animal control for New York City, and MacDonald eventually began to work in field services as an ambulance driver. His job entailed picking up injured animals, rescuing trapped animals, and rounding up strays. By the time MacDonald became a humane law enforcement agent in 1986, he had over a decade of intensive, hands-on experience working with animals. Law enforcement training followed, including learning how to safely handle the

Smith and Wesson .38 caliber revolver he was issued. While ASPCA agents had a long history of carrying firearms, mostly to humanely kill injured horses, their frequent forays into dangerous neighborhoods in pursuit of animal cruelty suspects increasingly required the weapons for their personal protection. Agents have had some close calls while working in the field, but to date no agent has ever fired his weapon at a person.

The ASPCA Humane Law Enforcement department has generally modeled its practices and appearance on the New York City Police Department. This includes similar uniforms and cars as well as investigative practices. This gives the team credibility with both the public and the police officers they encounter. As police training has continued to evolve and improve, so has the training for ASPCA agents. Training practices have also been driven by the changes in the requirements for New York State Peace Officers, who go through the same training as the ASPCA agents. Now under the jurisdiction of the State Division of Criminal Justice Services, all peace officers in New York State are required to undergo forty hours of classroom training on laws, and an additional forty-seven hours in the use of firearms and deadly force. ASPCA agents then receive additional training in laws specific to animals in New York State and on how to handle and care for animals.

A significant development in the training of ASPCA agents has been greater emphasis on criminal-investigation skills. As a result, new agents more often have a background in some form of law enforcement rather than in animal handling, as was the case in MacDonald's day and Ryan's before him. In days past, agents would frequently negotiate a "sidewalk plea bargain" with someone obviously neglecting an animal. If the person were willing to relinquish ownership of the animal to the ASPCA, the agent would agree not to issue a summons, though with the promise to keep an eye on the individual in the future.

Twenty years ago, the goal was saving animals, not prosecution. The courts and prosecutors often were unfamiliar with the laws related to animals and, with heavy court calendars, paid scant attention to cases brought in by ASPCA agents. As a result, seizures and arrests were focused on the more serious problems. More recently, however, greater attention has been placed on prosecuting perpetrators, and hence the need for more extensive criminal-investigation skills. Dale Riedel, current senior vice president of Humane Law Enforcement, points out that animal cruelty cases are similar to homicide investigations. There is no statement from the victim. This requires the investigator to have good interrogation and interview skills. All agents attend a special training course on interviewing and interrogation. In addition, several of the agents have attended the same Criminal Investigation Course given to all New York City detectives. Suspects are typically interviewed on the street or in their residences. In some cases, individuals will come to the ASPCA to meet with investigators. Viewers of the hit television series *Animal Precinct* know that perpetrators will often admit their guilt under patient and persistent questioning. In many cases they are simply unaware or unconvinced that harming an animal is a crime.

In addition to training with New York City detectives, ASPCA agents work with them on some special investigations. The ASPCA is often called upon when joint city, state, and federal officers are investigating criminal activity in High Intensity Drug Trafficking Areas (HIDTA). The ASPCA's long history in investigating and prosecuting animal fighting proves invaluable here. In 1981, Christopher Hoff, the general counsel for the Humane Law Enforcement department wrote an influential manual, *Dog Fighting in America: A National Review*. Funded with a grant from the Geraldine Dodge Foundation, the manual was a thorough analysis of dogfighting in America at the time. Hoff based his work on surveys and interviews with over 11,000 humane society and law enforcement officials. He traced the nature and development of the "sport," including information on the promotion of stud dog breeding lines.

Several case histories of successful investigations are presented in the manual. One of the more intriguing cases occurred in Rochester, New York, in 1980. It must be remembered that although the vast majority of the ASPCA's law enforcement work takes place in New York City, the society's charter in 1866 empowered its agents to enforce the anticruelty law everywhere in the state. In this instance, after meeting with local citizens and officials concerned with the possible presence of a dogfighting ring in their city, Hoff asked Ronald Storm, a cruelty investigator for the Humane Society of Rochester and Monroe County, to do some initial investigations and follow-up on several possible leads. While working on these leads, Storm contacted Al White, an investigative reporter for WOKR, the ABC television affiliate in Rochester. Working together, and using many of the contacts that White had developed over the years while pursuing other stories, Storm and White compiled a substantial amount of background information, and contacted the ASPCA for help in following up with the investigation. Hoff assigned Special Investigator Allan Roman, a five-year veteran at the ASPCA and an experienced undercover investigator, to travel to Rochester to meet with Storm and White and evaluate the available evidence. Based on the material presented, including video of the dogfighters secretly filmed by White and his crew, the ASPCA launched an undercover investigation. Roman was given an assumed name and identity. He was set up in an apartment complete with a two-way mirror and hidden cameras. The Humane Society of Rochester and Monroe County provided a four-month-old pit bull puppy named Pete to be a decoy and help to establish Roman's bona fides.

Roman began to walk Pete around the neighborhood, and soon attracted the attention of several dogfighting suspects in the area. One of these was Franklin Morison, thought to be the top dogfight promoter in Rochester. Morison took a liking to Roman and Roman's enthusiasm to learn about dogfighting. Morison soon became Roman's mentor, urging patience in training Pete, advising Roman to feed him well, provide him with vitamins, and wait until he grew up. In the meantime, Morison explained how he got into dogfighting. While Morison had started out with some "local" dogs, it was not until he met the legendary dogfighter, promoter, and breeder, Maurice Carver, that he really began to understand what he was doing. He eventually got rid of all of his original dogs and purchased several dogs from Carver who were bred from champion bloodlines. Morison stressed to Roman the importance of good breeding so that the dogs had the "gameness" necessary to become champions.

Roman's relationship with Morison led him to Stephen Hardy, a boyhood friend of Morison's. Hardy was a pimp and drug pusher, and shared with Morison a keen interest in dogfighting. Roman won the confidence of both men, but soon had a problem to confront. Hardy wanted Roman to fight Pete against one of his young dogs. Roman declined, but Hardy persisted. Roman eventually won out, and Hardy challenged Morison to fight one of his young dogs, just for fun. After witnessing the brutality of this informal match, Roman found a way to "lose" Pete, so he would no longer be in danger of being drawn into a fight.

The time came when Roman believed that he had learned all that he could about local dogfighting activities. While it did not seem that there was a large-scale professional fighting ring in Rochester, there was a small group of dedicated aficionados, and Roman now had enough evidence to conclude the investigation. Meanwhile, there was also mounting concern that White's role in the investigation was beginning to jeopardize it. Apparently, White's discretion was limited, and he had told more than one person about the investigation, including Roman's landlady. The ASPCA had informed the New York State Police of the investigation when it began, and kept them up-to-date with regular progress reports. As Roman and Hoff were preparing to wind down the operation and arrest Morison, Hardy, and others who were involved, they discovered that Morison was also involved in selling drugs. This revelation led the state police to request that the investigation be extended to gather further information on drug sales. They assigned a young trooper, Kevin Daniels, to go undercover as Roman's friend. The appearance of Daniels, and the new interest in drugs, raised some suspicion in Morison. The ASPCA and the state police decided they had all they were going to get, and it was time to plan and stage the final raid.

On an agreed-upon afternoon, Roman and Daniels headed to Morison's home. Earlier in the day, arrest and search warrants had been obtained from the appropriate courts. Roman and Daniels were armed since it was known that Morison and Hardy also carried weapons. As they went up to Morison's home, two carloads of state troopers and ASPCA agents fanned out in the area to provide backup and secure evidence. Morison was arrested without incident, and while Hardy was not there at the time, he eventually surrendered to police as well. In addition to dogfighting equipment, the troopers confiscated Morison's .357 magnum revolver and several ounces of marijuana.

Dogfighting was not yet a felony in New York State, so Morison, found guilty of animal fighting charges, was fined $300, and Hardy $250. The most serious penalty for these convictions may have been the confiscation and loss of valuable dogs and thousands of dollars' worth of treadmills and other dogfighting equipment. Finally, not to forget Pete, later that year ABC-TV's *Those Amazing Animals* program named him Dog of the Year for his role in the investigation!

Hoff also documented that drugs, gambling, and firearms were frequently found in dogfighting venues. It is for this reason that ASPCA expertise is valued in HIDTA investigations. ASPCA agents are often able to detect the presence of dogfighting paraphernalia, providing clues on where other criminal activities may be found.

Greater public concern about the mistreatment of animals, as well as a growing body of knowledge linking animal cruelty with other forms of violent and abusive behavior, has resulted in more attention to the issue among law enforcement officers, prosecutors, and judges. Especially heinous acts of cruelty to animals are now felonies in many states, thanks to the legislative efforts of the ASPCA and other organizations. As a result, ASPCA expertise is in demand for training programs in New York City, elsewhere in New York State, and across the country. ASPCA staff present lectures on animal cruelty and relevant laws to recruits at the New York City Police Academy. Training classes are also given around the state to peace officers and cruelty investigators from other organizations. The effort has also expanded nationwide with seminars and classes for cruelty investigators, police officers, and prosecutors. In addition to training classes presented in person by ASPCA staff, continuing education classes are provided for law enforcement officials via the Internet.

Just in time to greet the new century, a British television production company developed *Animal Precinct*, a reality show that featured the society's humane law enforcement officers on patrol in the city's five boroughs. The show premiered on the Animal Planet cable network in June 2001, and was an instant hit. Fifteen thirty-minute episodes were aired the first season. Three months later, public interest in the ASPCA's "animal cops" skyrocketed, as news coverage of the 9/11 disaster often included the role that was being played by the society's uniformed officers—as well as other ASPCA departments. By its second season, *Animal Precinct* was one of the most highly rated programs on Animal Planet. Before long, series featuring the humane law enforcement departments in Detroit, Houston, Miami, San Francisco, and Phoenix joined the lineup. In comparing the programs, it becomes obvious that only the ASPCA officers in New York City are able to make arrests. Bergh's accomplishment in securing this authority from the New York legislature is as impressive today as it was in 1866.

In later seasons, episodes of *Animal Precinct* were expanded to sixty minutes. Now in its sixth season, a typical episode begins with officers investigating complaints. Just as in Bergh's day, many people simply don't know how to care for animals properly, and many more are unaware that the law requires them to provide food, water, shelter, and veterinary care for their pets. Sometimes education and a warning are sufficient, and a case is closed when substandard conditions are corrected. Other cases are much more serious, and officers either seize animals who are in imminent danger, or, if possible, persuade their owners to relinquish them to the ASPCA. Saving the animals is always the officers' first concern. Confiscated or relinquished animal victims, many of whom are near death from starvation or untreated medical conditions, are brought to Bergh Memorial Animal Hospital, where officers document their condition and injuries in consultation with staff veterinarians. This crucial step allows agents to build a solid case to bring to a district attorney for prosecution.

Once admitted to the hospital, the animals are brought back to a healthy state, if possible. Staff and volunteers walk the dogs and socialize both dogs and cats. Behaviorists in the Animal Placement department evaluate the dogs to make sure their temperaments make them suitable family pets. After that, the animals are placed for adoption. Meanwhile, the humane law enforcement officers have spoken to witnesses and gathered enough evidence to arrest the animals' original owners.

Each episode of *Animal Precinct* is a "crime to punishment" sequence that often encompasses several months in real time. Viewers who tune in to the show learn a great deal about what is involved in enforcing the animal cruelty law as well as about the mission and the day-to-day workings of the ASPCA. So many people who watch *Animal Precinct* have contacted the ASPCA about becoming an HLE officer themselves, that a special link, "So You Wanna Be an Animal Cop?" was placed on the ASPCA's Web site to handle the volume of inquiries. The link averages 10,000 to 15,000 hits a month on aspca.org, and an additional 1,200 to 1,500 hits a month on Animaland, the ASPCA's Web site for children.

In the fall of 2003, *Animal Precinct* was reaching an average of seven million viewers. Membership and donations grew as a result. From its inception, this was the opening sequence for *Animal Precinct*: "New York City … 8 million people … 5 million pets … 10 animal cruelty agents with full police powers…. Welcome to the Animal Precinct." One enthusiastic viewer was struck with the absurd imbalance between HLE officers and the number of pets needing protection, and came up with a unique idea. He made a gift to the ASPCA specifically to expand the reach of the Humane Law Enforcement department, and offered a challenge grant to stimulate others to earmark their donations for this purpose. In 2007 there were nineteen agents on staff, with more to come.

Agents like Bill Ryan and Cowboy Langdon were familiar figures in their day, and minor celebrities in their own right, but the reach of television has catapulted today's officers to something akin to fame. Although this sometimes can get in the way of their work, and their privacy away from the job, it has also done a great deal to increase public awareness of animal cruelty and the important, difficult work that the agents do.

In 2006, the ASPCA's modern Bergh's men and women pursued 4,191 cases of animal cruelty in New York City, made a record 103 arrests, and seized 299 animals in connection with their investigations. They processed more than 50,000 calls and 10,000 e-mails from the public during the year. The cops were also on the road during the year, training professionals in other states on how to recognize and respond effectively to animal cruelty.

Chapter 9

Advocating for Animals

Henry Bergh was the ASPCA's first lobbyist. In 1866, with a little help from his friends, he drafted "An Act for the More Effectual Prevention of Cruelty to Animals." Then he traveled to Albany, persuaded another friend to introduce the legislation while he "stopped for a few days" in the state capitol to twist some arms. Back in New York, he took pen in hand and fired off letter after letter to the most influential newspapers in the city, informing the public about the legislation, reminding them of how badly it was needed, and complaining about how long it was taking the state assembly to do its duty. Whether or not Bergh expected his readers to contact their elected representatives and ask them to vote for the bill isn't known. Since the telephone wouldn't be invented for another ten years, it's unlikely that like-minded citizens could have done so even if they'd been strongly inclined.

Through the years, Bergh returned to Albany with amendments to strengthen the state's anticruelty law and expand its protections to animals. Initially he was successful, but as enforcement of the law began to affect commerce and convenience in the city—and the privileged pursuits of hunting, racing, and sporting gentlemen—the path to success became bumpier. Within four years of the society's founding, enough toes had been stepped upon that there was a very formidable attempt made in the New York state assembly to repeal the law completely, thus putting the ASPCA out of action. It was at this time that Hon. Elbridge T. Gerry joined the society as (unpaid) counsel, and Bergh happily handed off to him "the larger questions of law." Gerry went to Albany and "opposed the bill with eloquence and spirit" while Bergh wrote letters to keep the press and public informed. One letter Bergh wrote was to Mrs. Mary E. Lord of the Buffalo SPCA, encouraging her to do what she could to let the legislature know how people in Buffalo felt about the matter. Buffalo came through with a petition led by former U.S. President Millard Fillmore, who had helped found the Buffalo "branch" of the ASPCA. Several other communities did the same. To Bergh's horror, the bill passed in the assembly, and he hastened to appeal to Governor Hoffman (a founder of the society) to veto it. This turned out not to be necessary as the bill was defeated in the Senate, though by only two votes. Thus within its first few years of existence, the ASPCA experienced both the highs and the lows of working with lawmakers.

After Bergh died, the ASPCA acquiesced to New York City's request that the society run the city's pounds and manage animal control, and for one hundred years, this obligation gradually consumed more and more of the society's efforts and resources. For much of the time, the leadership and staff alike turned their focus inward, expending their energies on doing the best job they could in New York City under very difficult circumstances. Legislative activity largely went to the back burner, although over the years the society did join with other groups in supporting legislation regarding the use of animals, specifically in the 1950s and 1960s, when the issue of humane slaughter was being debated, both on the national level and within New York State. Until the federal "lobby law" of 1976 was passed, allowing nonprofit organizations to spend twenty percent of resources on lobbying efforts, animal welfare organizations risked losing their tax-exempt status if they spent a nonspecific "substantial" amount of resources on lobbying efforts. This potential jeopardy no doubt contributed to the back-burner position of the political advocacy aspect of Bergh's legacy.

This began to change in the mid-1980s. The society's new president, John F. Kullberg, Ed.D., appointed by the board in 1978, was an academician with strong personal convictions about the legislative approach to bringing about positive changes for animals. Soon the ASPCA had part-time lobbyists in Albany and in Washington, D.C. Attorney Lisa Weisberg was working in the society's legal department at the time, handling routine in-house corporate legal issues such as employee disputes, humane law enforcement powers, and wills and estates in which the ASPCA had an interest. When the then-current legislative session in Albany ended in 1990. Weisberg was tapped to work on state legislation full-time when the next term began. Over a few years' time, it became obvious that a part-time presence in the nation's capital was not enough to be effective. In 1996 Weisberg was asked to head up a new legislative services department for the society. She named the new department Government Affairs and Public Policy and increased the staff in Washington to three full-time employees, whose job was to monitor, initiate, and lobby for federal legislation to protect animals. Weisberg replaced herself in Albany with an experienced state lobbyist and then, as resources were made available, brought four additional state lobbyists on board in regions of the country where the ASPCA had large numbers of members who could be counted on to write the letters and make the telephone calls that are critical to the success of any legislative effort.

Although not so long ago in years, the mid-1990s now seem like the Dark Ages in terms of technology. So while Weisberg's department set up a Legislative Action Team for members who signed up to receive "alerts" when their help was needed to support or oppose bills in their statehouses or in Congress, this was wholly accomplished by what now is called "snail mail." Weisberg remembers stuffing envelopes and running them through a postage meter into the wee hours on more than one occasion. It wasn't long, however, before more and more members and supporters purchased their own personal computers and were able to go to the ASPCA's Web site, itself still quite primitive, to receive information about pending legislation in a more timely manner. A few years later, the Legislative Action Team morphed into today's Advocacy Brigade, which is Web-based and customized for individual members. When a member or supporter submits his or her address, "the system" generates a pre-written letter that is e-mailed to all his lawmakers in a matter of seconds. (Interestingly, legislators report that nothing really has replaced the importance to them of a handwritten letter or personal telephone call from a constituent.)

Following the terrorist attacks on the World Trade Center and the Pentagon on September 11, 2001, the ASPCA decided to close its Washington, D.C., office for the time being. All eyes in Washington and the nation were focused on Homeland Security and the War on Terror, suggesting that the coming years would not likely be favorable ones for animal-welfare legislation. But in the short period of time that the society had a Washington office, the team was very productive. The staff there helped to ensure that amendments to the Animal Welfare Act included exercise for dogs and psychological enrichment for primates in laboratories. They spearheaded the passage of two important pieces of federal legislation: the Pet Ownership in Public Housing Act (1999), which makes it illegal for anyone in federally assisted housing to be denied the opportunity to keep companion animals; and the Safe Air Transport for Animals Act (2000), which requires airlines to report all losses and deaths of companion animals shipped by air and mandates training of cargo handlers in animal-handling techniques. The Washington office was also instrumental in passing the Chimpanzee Health Improvement,

Maintenance, and Protection (CHIMP) Act (2000), which provides sanctuary for chimpanzees no longer being used for research. In addition to promoting these positive legislative actions, it was almost as important for the staff to monitor a wide range of legislative proposals, ensuring that those that would have a deleterious impact on animals were defeated.

Although the Washington office had closed, the ASPCA's regional legislative staff continued to work hard on statewide issues related to animals. For example, new state laws in 2005 that were drafted by ASPCA staff included low-cost spay/neuter in Illinois, mandated fingerprinting for animal abusers in New York, the protection of dogs in pick-up trucks in Connecticut, a requirement for cross-reporting human and animal abuse in Tennessee, disaster planning to include service animals and household pets in Louisiana, and the prohibition of "heart shot" euthanasia in California.

In late 2006, two of the ASPCA's legislative specialists participated in an electronic educational event. Hundreds of shelter employees, animal behaviorists, policy specialists, lawyers, government officials, and members of the media from across the country logged on to a public-safety "webinar" called "Dangerous Dogs—Is Canine Profiling Effective?" Sponsored by PetSmart Charities and taught by two attorneys from ASPCA Legislative Services, the Web-based seminar provided lifesaving information on the root causes of dog attacks and how to craft effective dangerous-dog laws to protect the public. It also addressed the rights of responsible dog owners and highlighted the ways in which dogs suffer as a result of breed-specific policies, which target specific breeds deemed to be dangerous, regardless of an animal's individual temperament.

Just a week after the webinar, the city commission of Emporia, Kansas, examined its vicious-dog ordinance at the request of a resident concerned about so-called "notorious breeds." Fortunately, city commissioners had attended the webinar and were equipped with information to make logical, not knee-jerk, policy decisions regarding the dogs in their community. As a result, the legislators rejected breed-specific legislation targeted at pit bulls.

The "Dangerous Dogs" webinar is just one of the many ways that the ASPCA legislative team reaches out to public and private groups across the country to educate those involved in animal welfare on the importance of sound animal protection laws. By the end of 2006, animal advocacy efforts across the ASPCA were impressive: 47 state bills drafted, testimony given at 125 hearings, 201 advocacy alerts sent out, and 230,000 letters sent to lawmakers in response to federal legislation. The Advocacy Brigade increased to half a million members.

Chapter 10

Working with Others

One of the ASPCA's most enduring contributions to the long-term benefit of animals may have been its role in inspiring the formation of thousands of other groups that have the protection of animals as their mission. Shortly after the formation of the ASPCA, societies modeled closely on the ASPCA sprang up in cities throughout the country.

Once Henry Bergh showed the way, others followed his example in tapping the wellspring of concern for animals, and the urge to reform. While Bergh's vision was broad, the day-to-day work required in New York City made it difficult for him to do more than make brief forays to other cities to encourage and cajole these groups. In turn, groups in other cities were heavily burdened with the needs of their own communities. In 1877, John G. Shortall of the Illinois Humane Society, along with Massachusetts SPCA's George Angell, Henry Bergh, and other leaders met in Cleveland, Ohio, to consider issues that required a broader, national perspective. This led to the formation of the American Humane Association (AHA). It was envisioned to be an organization that would coordinate the work of various local and regional humane groups in order to focus attention on issues with national importance. Bergh and the ASPCA had already been successful advocating for the passage of federal legislation in 1873 that provided some protection for livestock being shipped by rail. The newly formed AHA would continue advocacy in this arena, pushing for additional improvements that would eventually be passed in 1906.

Bergh's well-publicized rescue in 1874 of the child Mary Ellen Wilson, led many humane groups to add a child-protection role to their animal protection activities. They did not follow Bergh's example of forming a separate organization to pursue the child protection work. Despite Bergh's protestations that combining the two functions in one organization would result in one or both being slighted, AHA would accept and support both roles for humane groups. For many years AHA publications and conferences featured articles and presentations that ranged from fur trapping to child labor laws and lynchings, to the proper care of dogs and horses being used during WWI.

One of AHA's best-known contributions to the American lexicon was the initiation in May 1915 of "Be Kind to Animals Week." Celebrated each year since, it generally focuses attention on the things that children can do to protect animals.

For many people, their most likely contact with an AHA program would come through the cinema. Since 1941, the AHA has had a formal agreement with the film industry to inspect and oversee the use of live animals in films. If you sit through to the credits of a film, polishing off the last of your Goobers and popcorn, you will likely see the AHA logo with the assurance, "no animal was harmed in the making of this film." Over time, AHA's role as an association of humane societies has declined, though it continues to function as a humane organization with headquarters in Denver, Colorado, still combining the child and animal protection programs.

In 1954, a small group of AHA staff, dissatisfied with the organization's focus on animal sheltering—and its lack of attention and urgency toward vivisection, wildlife protection, and other issues—broke off to form the National Humane Society. The name was soon changed to Humane Society of the United States (HSUS). HSUS grew substantially over the years, and is now the largest of the humane groups in the United States.

In the ensuing years, the ASPCA, HSUS, AHA, and the Massachusetts SPCA (MSPCA) have worked together on a variety of different campaigns and efforts. In 1990, under the leadership of the ASPCA, HSUS, and MSPCA, a document entitled *Joint Resolutions for the 1990s by American Animal Protection Organizations*, was drafted. It was something of a manifesto, establishing an agenda for animal protection groups to share. Its introduction stated:

In order to establish the 1990s as a decade of rapid progress in diminishing the pain and suffering that billions of animals experience each year in laboratories, on farms, in the wild, as pets, in sports and entertainment, in exhibits and work situations, the undersigned humane organizations representing millions of concerned American citizens, have adopted the following Resolutions to promote and guide both individual and joint efforts on behalf of these animals who are so much in need of our immediate and compassionate care and protection.

What followed were a series of topics that described the major issues confronting laboratory animals, farm animals, wild animals, companion animals, and exhibition and work animals, as well as efforts that would be made to address the concerns. Leading the resolution was a statement on nonviolence. At a time when some individuals were advocating direct action against institutions that caused the death and suffering of animals, the Joint Resolutions made a clear statement that violence was not acceptable:

WHEREAS the foundation of the animal protection movement is that it is wrong to harm others; and
WHEREAS threats and acts of violence against people and willful destruction and theft of property have been associated with the animal protection movement; therefore, be it
RESOLVED that we oppose threats and acts of violence against people and willful destruction and theft of property.
RESOLVED that we shall energetically work to reduce, as rapidly as possible, the massive pain and suffering of billions of animals through nonviolent means.

The Joint Resolutions appeared as a two-page spread in the *New York Times* on January 29, 1991. They were signed by John Kullberg, Ed.D., president of the ASPCA, John Hoyt, D.D., president of the HSUS, and Gus Thornton, D.V.M., president of the MSPCA. Their signatures were followed by a list of 101 other humane groups that were committed to the resolutions.

Few people probably remember the resolutions, but they were the product of long and spirited meetings among the leaders of the three lead organizations. Their publication in the *Times* was something of a watershed in terms of visibility and clarity. Many things have changed since their publication. Significant progress has been made on some of the issues identified. Extensive research has yielded a number of alternative methods for toxicity testing; the euthanasia of unwanted pets in animal shelters is generally declining; and some major zoos have decided to eliminate their elephant exhibits due to concerns about the welfare of the animals—all topics addressed in the resolutions.

In 1993, what was sometimes known as the "Big Four"—the ASPCA, HSUS, AHA, and MSPCA—put their collective efforts behind a national Year of the Cat. All four organizations distributed the same T-shirts, coffee mugs, and bumper stickers adorned with a special Year of the Cat logo, and proclaimed the same message in their publications and other materials:

WHEREAS: Increasingly, people enjoy cats as companions with whom they share their homes and their lives; and

WHEREAS: Human beings have a responsibility to safeguard the well-being of all living creatures; and

WHEREAS: Cat owners' failure to act responsibly in caring for and sterilizing their pets has caused the overpopulation of cats to reach a crisis level; and

WHEREAS: Cats currently receive less protection under the law, less care, and less respect as a species than they deserve,

NOW, THEREFORE: In an effort to encourage the consideration of cats as sentient creatures worthy of our respect, compassion, protection, and careful stewardship, we hereby proclaim and pronounce the year Nineteen Hundred and Ninety-Three to be:

THE YEAR OF THE CAT and through the programs of our organizations, we will strive to improve the care, welfare and status of cats.

Many animal shelters across the country joined in the Year of the Cat campaign and used the platform provided by the joint effort to promote cat adoptions and spay/neuter programs. While this campaign may not have been the crucial event that turned the tide in terms of cat welfare in the United States, it did mark a point when shelters took a moment to rethink some of their practices and place greater emphasis on activities that would benefit cats.

Even though shelters seemed to be constantly dealing with a flood of unwanted animals, little effort was made to understand more fully the nature of the pet overpopulation question. Through the 1970s and 1980s, several conferences were held to discuss pet overpopulation, and how to deal with it. These conferences frequently ended with general agreement that groups would need to work together, and that more data were needed to develop effective interventions. In 1992, what might have been just one more such conference was organized in Minnesota by Dr. Patricia Olson from the University of Minnesota, and Dr. Mo Salman of Colorado State University. This meeting gathered representatives from the animal-shelter world, veterinarians, and dog and cat fanciers. The energy that developed during that meeting led to a second meeting, and from this would evolve the National Council on Pet Population Study and Policy (NCPPSP). Known simply as the National Council, the original organizations comprising its membership included:

- American Animal Hospital Association
- American Humane Association
- American Kennel Club
- ASPCA
- American Veterinary Medical Association
- Association for Veterinary Epidemiology and Preventive Medicine

- Cat Fancier's Association
- Humane Society of the United States
- Massachusetts SPCA
- National Animal Control Association

Whereas other meetings on pet overpopulation had not led to any sort of follow-up, the National Council became a dynamic organization with each constituent group bringing substantial skills and resources to the table. Considerable diplomacy was required, as some of the participating groups had longstanding suspicions regarding other participants. One of the first issues to be debated was the topic of study. Not all of the members agreed with the use of the term "pet overpopulation." As a result, the original mission stated for the National Council was "to gather and analyze reliable data that further characterize the number, origin and disposition of pets (dogs and cats) in the United States; to promote responsible stewardship of these companion animals; and based on data gathered, to recommend programs to reduce the number of unwanted pets in the United States."

The single thread that held the mission and the National Council together was the agreement that reliable data were needed, and that the groups involved could provide the National Council with the resources required to accomplish that mission. The key strategy was to study the death of animals in animal shelters as if it were a disease, and to collect the information needed to evaluate the risk factors for relinquishment and euthanasia. Research projects were designed and carried out to determine the reasons why animals are relinquished to animal shelters and how many animals enter shelters each year. A household survey was conducted to evaluate the movement of animals into and out of American households. Results of these studies were published in the peer-reviewed *Journal of Applied Animal Welfare Science* (*JAAWS*). Among them: There is a wide variety of reasons why animals are relinquished and no simple solution to the problem; a variety of methods was needed to reduce the surplus of animals, including reducing production, enhancing adoptions, returning lost pets to owners, and helping to keep adopted animals in their homes. The studies have been widely cited and have been used by shelters to develop programs to reduce the relinquishment of pets.

Various ASPCA staff have held leadership positions at the National Council from its earliest days. Stephen Zawistowski, executive vice president, National Programs; Julie Morris, senior vice president, National Outreach; and Pam Burney, vice president, Shelter Services, have all served terms as president of the National Council. Darlene Larsen, Midwest regional manager, Shelter Outreach, has served on the board of directors.

As relationships among animal sheltering organizations were improving in one area, they were growing strained in another. In 2004 a number of leaders in the animal shelter field gathered in Palo Alto, California, to discuss differences in opinion and misunderstandings related to the so-called no-kill movement. Much of the concern was driven by frequently fiery rhetoric that some shelters killed animals, but other animal shelters chose not to kill animals. Counterstatements said that "no-kill" shelters were a ruse, and were only able to avoid killing animals by closing their doors to homeless animals. Rich Avanzino, president of Maddie's Fund, a family foundation founded in 1999 and dedicated to making the United States a no-kill nation, helped to organize the meeting, knowing that all shelters share the goals of reducing the numbers of unwanted animals and eliminating the need to euthanize animals who could be placed in new homes. The results of agreements reached at this meeting have been published as the *Asilomar Accords*, named for the conference center that hosted the meeting. Ed Sayres, then and current president of the ASPCA, was a leader in hammering out the doctrine that would be espoused in the *Accords*, and the ASPCA was one of the first organizations to sign on to them. The *Accords* have three main parts:

- Guiding Principles to govern the interpretation of the statistics and the relationships among individuals and organizations involved with animals shelters.
- Consensus definitions that use nonjudgmental terminology to define various classes of dogs and cats who enter a shelter, and their disposition.
- A standard set of formulas for calculating the annual "live release rate," or fraction of animals entering into the shelter/rescue system of a community who are placed in new homes, returned to their owners, or transferred to other shelters or rescue groups.

The *Asilomar Accords* reflect the working philosophy of Ed Sayres, and the guiding policy of the ASPCA: that people working to help animals benefit from accurate, transparent data, and that different organizations working together in a community must develop respectful relationships. These two principles are bedrock in the bold initiative that the society launched in 2006, called ASPCA Mission: Orange. It is a collaborative program to establish humane communities all around the United States.

Bucolic Brewster, New York, is home to Green Chimneys Children's Services. A residential, therapeutic facility, it is dedicated to healing troubled children. The unique feature of Green Chimneys is that the therapeutic milieu includes animals. Founded by Sam and Myra Ross in 1947 on a 200-acre farm campus, it provides care for children with severe emotional and mental needs. In addition to the one hundred residential students on campus, the seventy-five day students are provided with a full array of psychological and counseling services. These therapies are interwoven with multiple opportunities to interact with animals on the farm.

The ASPCA has been a partner with Green Chimneys since the mid-1980s. Livestock seized during humane law enforcement investigations are often sent to Green Chimneys for placement. Pigs, horses, cows, goats, chickens, and other animals are among those lucky enough to live at least part of their lives in a hospitable environment. In one cruelty case that was featured on *Animal Precinct*, the reality show on the Animal Planet network that takes viewers on patrol with the ASPCA's humane law enforcement agents, a pair of swans beloved in their neighborhood had been brutally killed. Found near the dead animals was a clutch of eggs. HLE officers took the eggs to Green Chimneys, where they were incubated and safely hatched.

In many cases, Green Chimneys animals are recovering from physical and psychological neglect and trauma. The children there seem to sense that these animals have the same need for kindness and understanding that they do. Helping the animals to recover is incorporated into the treatment programs for the children.

Beginning in 1988 the ASPCA began to work with Psychologists for the Ethical Treatment of Animals (PsyETA) on a variety of topics. The most visible contribution was to provide financial and editorial assistance with the publication of *Humane Innovation and Alternatives and Animal Experimentation* (*HIA*). *HIA* was an early attempt to bridge the divide between vivisection and animal welfare. It published articles presenting information that helped to enhance the welfare of animals in laboratories, and elsewhere. *HIA* was printed and distributed by PsyETA to a small but dedicated group of animal welfare scientists and humane advocates. It was not peer-reviewed, however, and as a result, had limited acceptance in the general scientific community.

To advance the field of animal welfare science, the ASPCA and PsyETA agreed in 1993 to develop a peer-reviewed journal dedicated to the field. A proposal was developed and sent to a dozen publishers of scientific journals. Lawrence Erlbaum Associates (LEA) responded, showing interest in the opportunity. LEA is a well-respected publisher, with a number of high-quality journals and significant books to its credit. Dr. Kenneth J. Shapiro of PsyETA (now the Animals and Society Institute) and Stephen Zawistowski met with Lawrence Erlbaum, founder of the publishing company, to discuss the philosophy that would guide the journal and the range of topics that might be acceptable for publication. It was decided that the publication would be named *Journal of Applied Animal Welfare Science* (*JAAWS*) and publish articles, commentaries, and brief research reports on methods of experimentation, husbandry, and care that demonstrably enhance the welfare of nonhuman animals. Submissions would be accepted in four general topic areas: companion animals, animals in the laboratory, zoo animals and wildlife, and farm animals.

Section editors were recruited from among the premier scientists working on animal welfare issues. Among those who have served as section editors are Marc Bekoff, University of Colorado; David Morton, the University of Birmingham, United Kingdom; Joy Mench, the University of California at Davis; and James Serpell, the University of Pennsylvania. Shapiro and Zawistowski have served as the coeditors of the journal since its inception. The first issue appeared in 1998, and the journal began its tenth volume in 2007. Papers published in *JAAWS* have covered topics ranging from studies of relinquishment at animal shelters, to conditions of zoos in Indonesia. Articles published in *JAAWS* are frequently cited by other researchers and have influenced the development of policy for animal welfare organizations.

The Alliance for the Contraception of Cats and Dogs (ACCD) was formed in 2000 by Drs. Stephen Boyle of Virginia Polytechnic Institute, and Henry Baker and Brenda Griffin of the Scott-Ritchey Research Center of Auburn University. It was an informal organization of veterinarians, scientists, and others interested in pursuit of the "holy grail" of pet population management: a drug that would render dogs and cats sterile. While spaying and neutering of pets had helped to slow the tide of unwanted pets in some parts of the country, it had been the dream of many people working in animal welfare to have an inexpensive drug that could be given to pets. Two international conferences were sponsored by the ACCD bringing researchers and animal welfare advocates together to discuss and evaluate progress in the field.

After the second conference, held in 2004, a small group of people felt that it was time to organize a more formal group to pursue this dream. The ACCD was incorporated as a 501(c)3 nonprofit organization in 2006, with the stated mission of "expediting the successful introduction of nonsurgical sterilization for dogs and cats." This is an ambitious effort—experts estimate that it would take $10 million to bring a product from the stage of basic laboratory research to a final product approved for use by the Food and Drug Administration.

The ASPCA, already deeply committed to the importance of spaying and neutering pets, also recognizes the value of newer products that would make the sterilization of pets easier and less expensive. Given the ASPCA's history of investing in innovation, it is not surprising that the organization became the first significant supporter of the ACCD, providing more than $100,000 in grants in both 2006 and 2007. The support in 2006 was used to help defray the expenses of a third international symposium held in Alexandria, Virginia. It may indeed take a decade to achieve the goal envisioned. However, when you are already more than 140 years old, you have the time and experience to plan for the future.

In the years following the ASPCA's exit from animal control in New York City, there was a void in terms of overall strategy and tactics for taking on the homeless animal problem in the city. Activists finally came to realize that euthanasia of animals in the shelters had not been the sole result of the ASPCA's policies. The Center for Animal Care and Control, the new animal control agency formed in 1995, was underfunded. There was a big problem to tackle and limited resources available. In 2000 the Bar Association of the City of New York's Committee on Legal Issues Pertaining to Animals sponsored a conference—"Cats, Dogs, and Public Policy." Including ASPCA representatives, it brought together speakers from around the country familiar with various efforts to address pet population issues. The report from that conference attracted the attention of the newly elected mayor, Michael Bloomberg. Jane Hoffman—an attorney and one of the founders of the committee—met with the mayor's office. With the support of the mayor, she set out to form a coalition of New York City animal shelter and rescue groups to organize a coordinated effort to reduce and then eliminate the euthanasia of adoptable pets in New York City. The ASPCA was one of the six founding members of what became the Mayor's Alliance for New York City's Animals. In addition to providing visibility and logistical assistance to the Mayor's Alliance, the ASPCA provided seed money for many of its early activities. The stated goal of the Mayor's Alliance was to make New York City "no-kill" by 2008. In December 2002 the group signed a historic memorandum of understanding with the mayor's office declaring this goal, and the mayor's support of the effort.

The project clearly would require a substantial infusion of resources to make significant progress. The Mayor's Alliance set out to obtain a major grant from Maddie's Fund to provide the financial wherewithal to accomplish its ambitious goal. Maddie's Fund proposals require a substantial amount of background information, baseline statistics, and evidence of a well-organized community effort to carry out a plan to create a no-kill community. In May 2004 the ASPCA stepped to the plate, pledging $5 million to support the Mayor's Alliance over the next five years. This commitment by the ASPCA was instrumental in paving the way for a Maddie's Fund grant of $15.5 million over a seven-year period. The grant from Maddie's Fund will support adoption programs run by the Mayor's Alliance through its now more than one hundred participating organizations. It will also support increased spay/neuter programs through an agreement with the New York City Veterinary Medical Association. The ASPCA has continued to provide a variety of logistical services to the Mayor's Alliance, in addition to participating in and promoting its many adoption events. The ASPCA mobile adoption unit is always a stellar attraction at these events. The ASPCA has also taken on a substantial commitment to support increased spay/neuters of New York City pets. Its thirty-seven-foot-long mobile medical vans, which can sterilize twenty-five dogs and cats a day, visit dozens of neighborhoods and offer low-cost sterilization surgeries to pet owners unable to travel to veterinary offices, or unable to afford the procedure for their pets. Progress is being made, and in 2006, for the first time in New York City's history, more animals were adopted from shelters than euthanized.

Chapter 11

Humane Education

Early activities and stories about the ASPCA often featured the importance of teaching children to be kind to animals. In the society's annual report for 1868, there was a report on Henry Bergh's lectures during the year, and most of them were to groups of children. A beautiful illustration was reprinted of Bergh speaking to children at the Five Points House of Industry (Five Points being the city's most desperate neighborhood, as depicted in the 2002 film, *Gangs of New York*). The illustration showed Bergh surrounded by young children, all with one hand raised. The legend for the illustration read, "Raise your right hand if you will never harm a dumb animal."

Bergh was especially touched by letters from children that espoused their support for the ASPCA and his efforts. While the newspapers of the day frequently featured his letters with their soaring rhetoric castigating those who mistreated animals, few people saw the more gentle side of Bergh. When "Isabelle" wrote to him from Bethlehem, Pennsylvania, in 1879, she included twenty-five cents in her letter. Bergh's response acknowledged her donation. "As for your gift ... in as much as it represents your sympathy with the cause of humanity, and your affectionate tenderness towards dumb animals, I appreciate it just as much as though it were thousands of dollars. I have seen the time when just such moral support as you have sent me was worth more to me than all the gold in the Bank of England." He responded to another young girl, beginning his letter, "Your sweet little letter to me is as welcome as the early breath of spring."

Bergh was known to take time from his busy schedule to visit schools and orphanages to speak to children, trusting that their generation would mature and overcome the many cruelties inflicted upon animals. These education efforts remained an informal part of the ASPCA's work during

Bergh's lifetime, and for some years afterward. In 1894, President John Haines made a point of noting that the value of the society's educational work could not be estimated in figures, "nor perhaps in any other way." The previous year, the ASPCA published "Kindness to Animals: A Manual for Use in Schools and Families," which it distributed for four cents a copy.

Special agents of the society gave impromptu lectures on the proper care of animals to children who may have gathered to observe them while they worked at inspecting horses. Groups of children were able to tour the stables, hospital, or shelters. Families with children were always welcome to visit the shelters and consider adopting a family pet. These tours often included a brief lecture on the responsibilities of having a pet, with some emphasis on the importance of having a dog licensed to ensure that if lost, it could be returned to the family.

In addition to these direct contacts with children and adults regarding the proper care of animals, the society also produced a wide variety of publications for distribution. One very popular and important item was a manual called "Title XVI of the Penal Code," which included laws and penalties related to animals. Additional material included information on how to evaluate the condition of horses, identifying common illnesses and injuries. Leaflets on the cruelty in dehorning cattle and docking the tails of horses were published, as well as one that exposed the destruction of birds for the fashion industry.

An Education department was officially formed in 1916. The society now had a dedicated staff to develop educational materials for children. The new department moved quickly to establish both its visibility and impact. The outreach efforts in that first year included 88 lectures to public schools, reaching 34,692 students; the creation of Young Defender's League clubs that enrolled an additional 23,470 children; and public lectures that reached more than 37,000 adults. By 1918, wealthy land developer and philanthropist General Horace W. Carpentier gave a gift of $100,000 to Columbia University, where Henry Bergh had matriculated for a short time, to create a foundation in Bergh's name "to inculcate a spirit of kindness and consideration toward the lower animals." While the foundation has since "disappeared" into the bureaucracy of an Ivy League institution, several books on humane education and the history of the movement were published under its auspices. One such text, *The Humane Movement in the United States, 1910–1922*, by William J. Shultz, Ph.D., was published in 1924.

A compulsory humane education bill was introduced in New York State in 1917 and was finally enacted in 1947. It mandates weekly instruction in the humane care and treatment of animals in all public elementary schools. Unfortunately, the law has never been enforced.

The society's 1919 annual report included "Ten Rules for the Treatment of Animals." While parts of it are dated, the general tenor of the rules set a standard of care that would be appropriate to emulate today.

I. No one has a right to keep animals, either for use or for pleasure, unless he is able and willing to provide them with whatever is necessary for their health and happiness.

No animal can be healthy or happy unless it is kindly treated, comfortably lodged, regularly fed, supplied with water, and afforded opportunities of recreation.

II. Gentle treatment is due to all animals, and need not interfere with firmness in governing them. Animals are often thought to be ill-tempered or obstinate when they are really suffering from some pain or irritation of which we do not perceive the cause, but which may be soothed by patience and quietness.

If you try to find out what is the matter with an animal before you punish him, you will probably find out that there is no reason to punish him.

Be careful to remove anything that causes fear. Animals are often terrified by things that men hardly observe. If they are punished, their terror is only increased. Nothing will quiet them so soon as gentle talk and caressing.

Kindness will win the confidence of any animal, and an animal which confides in its keeper is easily managed.

If you want your horse to work well, take good care that his harness does not chafe him.

III. All animals require the sunshine, and their dwellings should have a southerly or westerly aspect, if possible; but they should always have access to shade when they desire it.

Stables, sheds, coops and cages should be well drained, well lighted and well ventilated, but never draughty.

Different animals require different temperatures. A humane owner ought to learn the degree of heat and cold which the animal is enabled by nature to endure.

Every stable, yard, cage, kennel and bed should be kept thoroughly clean.

IV. Every animal should have as much solid food daily as it will eat up clean, but no more than it will consume. Stale food is unwholesome. It should be removed early in the morning, and replaced by a fresh supply.

Nocturnal animals should be fed at sunset.

Be careful to give all animals as much variety of food as possible, and let it be as nearly as possible the food which the animal would use in a state of nature. Animals which are regularly fed on grain ought to have frequent supplies of green food.

V. Every animal should have an abundant supply of pure water for drinking.

Vessels used for food or water should be washed daily, and wiped dry before refilling. Iron troughs or plates lined with porcelain are best, being clean, cheap and durable.

VI. Bathing is necessary to the health and comfort of many animals. Cage-birds ought to be allowed to bathe daily, and a separate vessel, adapted to their size, should be supplied for that purpose. Some birds delight in dust baths. A working horse should be allowed every day to roll on the grass, or, better, perhaps, on sawdust.

VII. Animals, as well as men, are happier and better for reasonable recreation. Whenever it is possible, they should have it. The horse should be allowed an opportunity to run at large. Dogs, especially in cities, should be taken out to run freely. Even cage-birds are immensely pleased if they are allowed to leave the cage for an hour or so every day.

VIII. When an animal is sick, see that it is kept quiet and unmolested and that its treatment is unusually gentle.

IX. When it is certain that an animal will die, always secure the services of a humane and experienced person to destroy it in the quickest and least painful way; and when it dies, never fail to bury it at once.

X. Try to make the world as happy a world as possible for any of God's creatures that may happen to be in your charge.

A publication for children was developed, *Our Animal Friends*, which provided information on animal care, stories about animals, and general acknowledgement that being kind was honorable and highly desired. Young Defenders received copies of the publication, and met in small groups to discuss how they could help animals. They were encouraged to be kind to stray animals and help wildlife. They were discouraged from collecting eggs from birds' nests, a popular hobby at the time. Children who became leaders of their small groups were named "captains." They were then given a pin with the ASPCA seal on it. One small boy, upon receiving his pin remarked, "Is this an angel on the pin? That's the first time I ever saw an angel doing anything. Usually they only sing."

In the 1920s the society developed a relationship with the Maxwell Training School for Teachers in Brooklyn. Working with faculty from the school, several lesson plans were developed for teaching humane education. Educator Frances Elizabeth Clarke, among others, anticipated the modern "blended curriculum" movement and edited the *Lessons for Teaching Humane Education in Elementary Schools* series. In 1925 Clarke and Emma L. Johnston, Maxwell School principal, produced the first in the series "Plays and Pageants." The booklet included eight short plays designed to allow children to act out scenarios in which they could take on the role of an animal or of someone responsible for the care and treatment of animals. Additional titles included lessons correlated with nature, music, and poetry. The language reflected the values of the day, and it was common for some of the material to have a religious feel. A poem by Meta Buermeyer reflects this approach:

> Be Kind to Living Things
>
> Little children, bright and fair,
> blest with ev'ry needful care.
> Always bear this in mind,
> God commands us to be kind.
>
> Kind not only to our friends,
> those on whom our life depends.
> Kind not only to the poor,
> those on who poverty do endure.
>
> But in spite of form or feature,
> kind to every living creature.
> Never pain or anguish bring,
> even to the smallest thing.

In 1927, the New York State Board of Regents appointed a Council on Character and Humane Education, and the ASPCA Humane Education director was named to serve. By this time, humane education had a quasi-official status within the New York City Department of Education. For a number of years the ASPCA Humane Education department coordinated with the New York City public schools, through the city education department's art division, to sponsor a poster contest. Thousands of entries were received annually, colorful expressions of children's thoughts on kindness toward animals. ASPCA shelters were decorated with the posters and the winning entries were placed on display in banks and other businesses throughout the city.

The 1920s and 1930s were a golden age for parades in New York City. Groups of workers, military detachments, and ethnic enclaves often took to the streets to celebrate their activities and solidarity. Not to be outdone, each year the city's education department sponsored separate "Boys Day" and "Girls Day" parades. Boys and girls would march with their schools, or with clubs they belonged to. A "Humane Education" division was one such grouping. Boys in knickers and knee socks proudly marched in formation to proclaim their support for the kind treatment of animals. The ASPCA soon developed summer programs that were presented at neighborhood playgrounds when school was out of session. Humane education was promoted as a way to reduce crime and promote peace.

One unique education effort by the society harkens back to its early focus on the horse. In 1933, ASPCA board member Alfred Maclay, who was active in the world of breeding and showing horses, donated a trophy for a junior riding championship in which young competitors are judged not only on their skill as riders but on their knowledge of horse care and the humane treatment of their mounts. Eligible juniors at shows across the country compete for points in any Maclay National Championship Qualifying Class throughout the show season, and riders with the most points are invited to compete at the National Horse Show in New York City each fall, at which the trophy is awarded. The "Maclay" eventually became the premier competition class for junior riders. The winner each year is considered the best junior rider in the country. Many Maclay winners have gone on to become world-class and Olympic equestrians. The Maclay trophy is still offered each year by the ASPCA. Winners receive a ribbon, a replica of the trophy, and a horse cooler blanket. In some years, the winner has received a scholarship.

In 1944, the ASPCA was at the forefront in offering a new kind of educational activity to the public: dog obedience training. The course was sponsored by the Education department, and teaching the classes was Blanche Saunders, already one of the foremost trainers in the country, who had herself been schooled by Mrs. Helene Whitehouse Walker, the Bedford Hills, New York, woman responsible for importing the new sport of dog obedience from England. The society's training course ran for ten consecutive weeks and was held at the Seventh Regiment Armory at Park Avenue and Thirty-fourth Street. The ASPCA offered some form of obedience training to the public off and on until the spring of 2005.

When the ASPCA was forced to move out of its location at Twenty-fourth Street and Avenue A in 1948, tremendous pressure was placed on the society's finances and operations. One benefit of the move, however, is that it provided the opportunity to expand the humane education programs. The new building at 441 E. Ninety-second Street was designed to include a humane education classroom and space for a small menagerie of animals used in education programs. The ASPCA quickly became a popular destination for scout troops and class field trips. Daytime classes and after-school programs at one point in time featured cage birds; small animals such as hamsters, mice, and guinea pigs; a dog and a cat; and more exotic creatures, including a boa constrictor, a gibbon, and a kinkajou, or honey bear. All of these animals had been rescued by ASPCA staff and given medical treatment at the ASPCA animal hospital before joining the Education department.

ASPCA junior members were allowed to help care for the department's animals, and Saturdays were reserved for this purpose. Many biologists, teachers, and veterinarians had their first real experience with animals as junior members working in the ASPCA Humane Education department.

An ASPCA "Arkmobile" was added in the 1960s to bring animals and the kindness message to communities and neighborhoods throughout New York City. In April 1968, the Arkmobile traveled to an event in Harlem sponsored by the African Humane Society. More than 500 children attended. The Arkmobile also served as the society's first mobile adoption unit. It made an appearance at the 1974 Empire Cat Show at Madison Square Garden and helped place twenty-three cats in new homes.

The ASPCA Humane Education department quickly adapted to new communication mediums. Staff were regular contributors to radio broadcasts, bringing information on responsible pet care and other important issues to the general public. In 1970 this included Dr. Leon Abrevaya from what was now the Bergh Memorial Animal Hospital, making regular appearances on Spanish-language television.

A number of different television shows chose to feature the ASPCA in one of their segments. The well-regarded ABC show, *Discovery*, came to the ASPCA in 1967 to film its activities and programs. Later that year, a TV producer paid the ASPCA $1,000 to film a pilot about the society's daily activities, with the intention of developing a regular television series focused on the work of the humane law enforcement agents. That show did not make it on the small screen, but the idea did have "legs," though it would wait until 2001 before Animal Planet would introduce the American public to *Animal Precinct*, the gritty reality series now in its sixth season. Even Walt Disney got into the act, negotiating for the film and television rights to *Fifty Years in the Doghouse*, Lloyd Alexander's 1963 story about ASPCA special agent Bill Ryan's more than fifty years working for the ASPCA. Disney never did produce a film version of the story, but it is intriguing to consider what might have happened if Bill Ryan's adventures had joined those of Davy Crockett and Daniel Boone. There may have been a theme song sung by children from coast to coast, perhaps a ride at Disney World featuring Ryan's beloved red-and-gold horse ambulance.

The ASPCA did venture into film production in the 1980s. Working with a grant from the Dodge Foundation, the Humane Education department produced three films with production company Varied Directions on important animal protection issues. The first film, *The Other Side of the Fence*, produced in 1988, considered the welfare of farm animals and highlighted concerns arising out of intensely confined husbandry practices. Crate-raised veal calves were the centerpiece of the film that coincided with the ASPCA's naming the veal calf its "animal of the year" in 1988. In 1989, a second film, *A Question of Respect*, looked at the use of animals in research and product testing, and included footage and comments provided by chimpanzee expert and advocate Jane Goodall. *The Price They Pay*, produced in 1990, presented issues associated with trapping and other practices that threaten wildlife. The three films were widely distributed to schools, and received several educational media awards. Also published at this time was *The Animal Rights Handbook: Everyday Ways to Save Animal Lives*, a Living Planet Press paperback that was described as an "instant classic." The ASPCA's president at the time, John F. Kullberg, Ed.D., wrote the book's foreword, and in 1991, a special edition was published to commemorate the society's 125th anniversary.

In 1990, the ASPCA coproduced *Where Have All the Dolphins Gone?* with California's Marine Mammal Fund. Narrated by actor George C. Scott, the film featured the undercover work of biologist and filmmaker Sam LaBudde. Posing as a cook, LaBudde went to sea on a tuna-fishing boat and captured horrifying images of dolphins being caught up and drowned in the nets intended for tuna, or mangled in the winch that hauls the nets onto the boat. The film premiered on the Discovery Channel during Earth Day specials on April 22, 1990. It became part of a national campaign that was joined by hundreds of animal welfare and environmental groups with the intent to reform the way tuna are netted. As part of the campaign, children wrote letters to request that schools not serve tuna in cafeterias until change came about. Eventually the tuna industry did change its methods of catching tuna, and the now familiar "Dolphin Safe" logo began to appear on canned tuna.

Another film developed in the 1990s was *Throwaways*, a series of vignettes that promoted spaying and neutering of companion animals to combat pet overpopulation. Tens of thousands of copies of the video were distributed by the ASPCA, and it is believed that it may be the most widely distributed humane education video of all time. A couple of years later, in 1993, *Rechazado* followed as a Spanish-language version of *Throwaways*.

Working with WILL television at the University of Illinois with a grant from the Kenneth A. Scott Trust, a series of three-minute pet care segments was produced and syndicated on public television in 2000. *Pet Check* was seen in major markets across the country and brought advice on how to pick a shelter pet, avoid dangers in hot and cold weather, and cope with the loss of a beloved companion animal.

In addition to films and television, the Humane Education department developed a series of curriculum packages, lesson plans, and other materials for teachers during the 1990s. The department continued the blended-curriculum approach first tried in the 1920s, which was once again a key approach in education theory. The first such product was *Web of Life*, which included an audiotape and photocopy masters for handouts. The program emphasized the connections between all living things and the important role that humans can play in helping to protect and preserve animals and the environment. One very popular exercise in the package was titled "Are They Guilty?" Introduced by a "radio news report" on the audiotape, it allowed students to play out a cruelty case against a couple who failed to provide proper care for their pets. While some students played the roles of the judge, jury, prosecutor, and of course the accused, other students played the mistreated pets. *Web of Life* was followed up in 1999 with *I Love Animals*, another integrated-curriculum package of lesson plans.

The inspiration to publish a Spanish-language curriculum package came out of a conference held at Green Chimneys Children's Services in Brewster, New York. The ASPCA has a history of collaboration on humane education activities with Green Chimneys, which is a residential, therapeutic center for at-risk children, where rescued and abandoned farm animals and wildlife are part of the treatment program. In the early 1990s, Green Chimneys and the ASPCA hosted a conference—"Diversity Issues in Humane Education"—bringing together experts from around the country. The results of that conference eventually led to the publication by the ASPCA of a Spanish-language humane education curriculum, *Yo Quiero a los Animales* (*I Love Animals*), a translation of the earlier English curriculum package of that name. Additional conferences were held at Green Chimneys in 2003 and 2007, weaving together the value that contact with animals can have for the emotional development of children, and how we can develop innovative ways to encourage kindness and caring in the young.

In the mid-1990s the department initiated what has become a well-received emphasis on children's literature. For years, publishers have mailed complimentary copies of children's books about animals to the

ASPCA. Some were good, with strong humane themes. Some were not so good. It seemed clear that students, parents, and librarians could use some guidance about the many books published for children. *Kids, Animals and Literature* was conceived as an annotated bibliography. ASPCA staff in Humane Education and several other departments took on the task of reading hundreds of children's books and writing descriptions of each book. Education majors at the Staten Island campus of St. John's University were enlisted to help. *Kids, Animals and Literature* has gone on to become a key resource for the education community. Librarians have written letters expressing special appreciation for the bibliography during Be Kind to Animals Week in May, when they are overwhelmed with requests for help from students preparing reports on helping animals.

The continued success and acceptance of the bibliography eventually evolved into the ASPCA Henry Bergh Children's Book awards for the best books about animals published for children each year. The first awards were presented in San Francisco in 2000 at the annual meeting of the American Library Association. Each year hundreds of books are received and reviewed by ASPCA staff. Dozens of people across the society read the books, grade them, and then meet in small groups to nominate finalists in different categories. The final judging committee has included two of the society's presidents—first, Dr. Larry Hawk, and now Edwin J. Sayres—and also Dr. Sam Ross, founder of Green Chimneys, and Charles Bergh, a descendent of Henry Bergh. Winning titles are authorized to have the coveted Henry Bergh Children's Book Award seal placed on the cover.

In 2001 the ASPCA launched Animaland (www.animaland.org), a Web site for kids who love animals. Featured content includes pet care information, cartoons, an animal encyclopedia, and *Ask Azula*, a popular column in which a blue-and-gold macaw answers kids' questions about animals. Animaland also features activities developed by ASPCA humane educators, and a section on hard-hitting issues in the animal-welfare world written in language that kids can understand. The site receives nearly 200,000 unique visitors every month, and in 2004 was honored with the Parents' Choice Gold Award and a WebAward for outstanding achievement in Web site development by the Web Marketing Association, Inc.

As part of the society's 140th anniversary celebration in 2006, a new award was inaugurated. The lifetime achievement award for children's literature is named for Roger A. Caras, a past president of the society and prolific author of books on animals. The ceremony in 2006 was held at the American Library Association conference in New Orleans. It was a dramatic event, as it also reunited ASPCA staff who had come to New Orleans in the wake of Hurricane Katrina to join in animal rescue efforts, with colleagues from the Louisiana SPCA. The crowd of authors, publishers, and animal professionals erupted in applause and a standing ovation when Norman Bridwell, the creator of the *Clifford, the Big Red Dog* series for Scholastic, Inc., came forward to accept the first Roger Caras Achievement Award and the accolades of his fans. In 2007, Caras's widow, Jill Caras, presented the second annual Roger Caras Achievement Award to Jean Craighead George at an evening program during the American Library Association conference in Washington, D.C. George, author of *My Side of the Mountain* and *Julie of the Wolves*, among other beloved children's books, was likewise greeted with a standing ovation.

Chapter 12

Humane Communities

From its very first days, the ASPCA has been an innovator, bringing new methods and technologies to bear in its mission to prevent cruelty. While Henry Bergh was alive, if something were needed yet didn't exist, the ASPCA founder invented it. He invented the horse ambulance to remove horses from the streets when they were too ill or injured to travel, and a sled to serve as a litter. To raise horses who had fallen into the river, or into excavations, he invented a sling to lift them back to safety. Bergh had a hand in the development and promotion of alternatives to shooting live pigeons for sport. The gyropigeon, glass balls, whirligigs, and eventually the "clay pigeon" were introduced, to the benefit of their live counterparts. And in a letter to the editor of the *New York Tribune* in 1869, it was revealed that Bergh innocently enough had invented another, treasured item that has survived to this day. In describing the invention, which was the sole purpose of the communication, the *Tribune* letter writer repeated the words he overheard Bergh saying, sotto voce, to his waiter in a lunchroom: "Will you please wrap these bits of chicken in a piece of paper? I want them for a hungry old dog of my acquaintance...."

Later, ASPCA veterinarians and staff improved in-hospital horse care by installing a track on the ceiling and attaching Bergh's sling. The combination allowed them to move equine patients safely into position. Bergh offered rewards for the best design of a railroad car to ship livestock long distances, for a more humane yoke for oxen, and for other improvements in husbandry. Many years later, the ASPCA patented the design for humane slaughter pens for large and small animals. Bergh was innovative, and in 1866, there was much still to be conceived of.

Innovations have occurred in many areas of the ASPCA's work. The Animal Poison Control Center is the only toxicology center in America geared to animals and staffed by veterinary toxicologists. In the late 1990s, the ASPCA partnered with Petfinder (www.petfinder.com) to introduce animal shelters and the public to online adoption searches. To facilitate use of the new technology, the ASPCA bought and distributed hundreds of digital cameras and gave them to animal shelters that agreed to post their pets on the Petfinder network. The ASPCA was the first animal shelter to use formal behavior evaluations on dogs, and is poised to introduce a national Web-based behavior helpline service. Also in the late 1990s, the ASPCA introduced Animed, a toll-free telephone pet-care information service with prerecorded advice on more than one hundred common issues. Animed was discontinued by the ASPCA in 2006. ASPCA staff edited the first textbook in the brand-new field of shelter medicine and are at work on a second. The ASPCA Humane Law Enforcement department—the nation's first to be empowered by legislative act to enforce a state's anticruelty laws—has begun to train law enforcement units across the nation in the skills they've developed over 140-plus years. The list goes on.

Since its founding, the ASPCA mission has been to provide effective means for the prevention of cruelty to animals throughout the United States. Henry Bergh did all he could to encourage other states and localities to establish societies similar to the ASPCA and in this way extend what he called the "humane and civilizing" benefits of the work. His dream was that every state and territory would have a society to prevent cruelty to animals. Then, he felt, his life would not have been in vain.

In 2007, the ASPCA launched an ambitious new program that dared to envision an American nation where every adoptable pet would find a loving home, and where all animals would be treated with compassion and respect. The name of the new program is ASPCA Mission: Orange.

ASPCA Mission: Orange (orange, which universally refers to lifesaving, is the society's new corporate color) targets specific cities across the country where it will focus intensive efforts to bring about immediate, measurable, and sustainable change for the community's animals. The initiative addresses the animals most at risk—i.e., shelter animals—by including and collaborating with leading community agencies and organizations to implement a save rate at or above seventy-five percent for unwanted pets entering shelters. Since each community has a different environment and needs, the ASPCA is collaborating with partners in each target community to develop the programs and resources that will be most effective in helping that specific community reach its goals. The ASPCA will commit funds (up to $600,000 in each city over three years), staff, extensive training, and a wealth of expertise. The ASPCA is also working closely with the Richmond SPCA of Richmond, Virginia, which will serve as a "learning laboratory" for ASPCA Mission: Orange communities, sharing resources and expertise through learning and exchange programs. First stops in 2007 were Austin, Philadelphia, Tampa, Gulfport–Biloxi, and Spokane.

Innovative programs to boost adoptions of shelter pets, and to expand anticruelty training and low-cost spay and neuter services, typify the services the ASPCA is helping to introduce and expand in the target communities. The idea is that because of the intensive focus and collaborative approach of Mission: Orange, many more animals will be saved, and fewer will ever get into a shelter in the first place. The partnerships in the targeted cities are expected to serve as a model to other communities across the country.

The program got off to a strong start. In Austin, the ASPCA pledged $300,000 as a lead gift to Animal Trustees of Austin to build roomy new Spay/Neuter and Wellness Clinics to replace their cramped, outmoded facility. Advanced anticruelty training for police and others on such topics as animal hoarding and "blood sports" such as dogfighting and cockfighting will provide further protection for animals, and a new spay and neuter program for feral cats at the Austin Humane Society will allow that agency to address the "prevention" part of its mission in a way that it had never been able to do before.

In Philadelphia, the next city to come online, a new operating room at the city's animal shelter, funded largely by a $150,000 ASPCA gift, will allow senior veterinary students at the University of Pennsylvania to sterilize an additional 1,200 dogs and cats ready to go out for adoption each year. Additionally, humane education in Philadelphia will get a big boost from a $30,000 ASPCA grant to the Pennsylvania SPCA to create an informational Web site targeted at teachers and schoolchildren throughout the state.

In Tampa, ASPCA Mission: Orange efforts include behavior-assessment training to complement shelter adoption programs and efforts aimed at curbing the problem of pet overpopulation, which is a key reason so many animals end up in shelters. In May 2007, the ASPCA and its partners in Tampa took over the Florida State Fairgrounds with approximately 300 homeless animals from twenty participating animal rescue groups. The Spring Pet Adoption Expo was a great success, as 170 cats and dogs found new homes that day—roughly three times as many as in similar events in the past. The ASPCA's Sherry Silk, manager of Southern Regional Outreach, orchestrated the event, and plans to do even better in 2008.

In Gulfport–Biloxi, the new state-of-the-art Humane Society of South Mississippi, funded in part with a $1 million gift from the ASPCA following the ravages of Hurricane Katrina, will take a three-pronged approach that includes counseling and education for new pet parents, low-cost spay and neuter services for some 15,000 pets a year, and expansion of The Love Train, which last year transported more than 1,200 animals to areas of the country where they can more easily be adopted. Expanded anticruelty training for three regional police departments will further aid animals in need.

Spokane was the latest beneficiary of ASPCA Mission: Orange involvement. Launched in May 2007, it was the first West Coast community to join the society's goal of a humane nation. Like the other target cities, Spokane and its community partners received a three-year commitment from the ASPCA.

Much of the inspiration for ASPCA Mission: Orange grew out of ongoing efforts in New York, where the ASPCA served as a founding member and provided a $5 million lead grant to the Mayor's Alliance for NYC's Animals. This public–private partnership, involving nearly one hundred animal welfare groups, is working to build a humane community in which none of the city's dogs and cats of reasonable health and temperament is killed merely because he or she lacks a home. The collaborative efforts are starting to pay off. In 2006, more than 20,000 animals were adopted into great new homes, and for the first time, more animals were saved than euthanized in the city's Animal Care and Control system.

In its intention to create an entire nation of humane communities, one community at a time, ASPCA Mission: Orange is a twenty-first century strategy to accomplish Henry Bergh's nineteenth-century dream.

Afterword

T here is a fine line between what is historic and what is hide-
bound, and managing a venerable organization like the ASPCA,
with its founder looking over your shoulder, requires finding a
balancing point between the two. On the other hand, asking, "What
would Henry do?" hardly qualifies as a strategic plan for the twenty-first
century. In seeking to explain why the ASPCA has endured for more
than 140 years, two primary reasons stand out. First, the society's
mission—to provide effective means to prevent cruelty to animals—has
never lost its power to call to and motivate compassionate people. Second, as times have changed, the society has been able to adapt, fulfilling
its historic mission in new ways.

Perhaps most significant has been the changing profile of the ASPCA's
staff and leadership. In the nineteenth century, when the motive power
of society stood on four strong legs, "Bergh's Men" were teamsters,
prized for their skill with horses. Bergh himself was an amateur, inventing
not only the organization but the field of animal protection in America.
He came to the work late in life, with no special skills or preparation,
making the most of his passion, perseverance, and social connections.

Unlike Bergh, the ASPCA's current president, Edwin Sayres, came to
the position with more than thirty years of experience in animal protection. He represents a generation of professionals who have made work in
this field a career vocation. Sayres began as a humane educator, later
served as president of St. Hubert's Giralda—a successful animal shelter in
New Jersey—moved on to lead the animal protection division of American Humane Association, from there went to PetsMart Charities, and
then spent several years as president of the San Francisco SPCA before
coming to the ASPCA in 2003. Thus Sayres brings to the task an

understanding of animal welfare issues and the day-to-day operations of an animal shelter, as well as a proven track record in managing a major nonprofit organization within a competitive charitable environment.

In contrast to Bergh's Men, the staff that Sayres oversees comprises professionals drawn from a variety of relevant fields. The majority are college graduates, and a significant proportion have advanced graduate degrees. In communicating with the society's members, supporters, and the public, Bergh and those who succeeded him at the helm relied on printed handbills and manuals, while Sayres and his team are pioneering the use of the Internet to deliver the message. The society has already embarked on the ambitious use of "Web 2.0" technology to support its animal-protection efforts: blogs, personal pages, text messaging, and video downloads have replaced Bergh's indefatigable pen. Convinced that near instant access to accurate information will be a critical tool in further enhancements to animal protection, the society has made important investments in the area of "knowledge management." This strategy paid significant dividends during the pet food recall crisis of spring 2007, allowing the ASPCA Animal Poison Control Center to track reports on exposures, correlate the reported symptoms with knowledge of suspected contaminants, and play a leading role in helping to untangle the mystery of what was causing so many pets to fall ill.

The ASPCA's board of directors has likewise continued to evolve. Current Board Chairman Hoyle Jones is a career human resources professional in the banking industry, and brings acumen in managing people and issues to his role. The board that he chairs includes a wide range of successful professionals spanning finance, law, veterinary medicine, and real estate, among other fields. No longer a male-only domain, the board now includes many women who hold significant leadership positions as committee chairs with significant involvement and input in program development and delivery. The board's fiduciary oversight has helped to ensure that the society has the resources it needs to fulfill its mission.

What has not changed since 1866 is the dedication that the ASPCA staff and board bring to their work. Whether responding to a cruelty complaint in Brooklyn, assisting hurricane victims in New Orleans, finding a home for a cat with special needs, or answering a child's e-mail about what to feed a pet hamster, there is a sense of commitment and concern that Bergh would still recognize. These activities *are* the heritage of care. This book is a look back at the society's history, but it is also a window to a future that promises to be as exciting and productive as the past.

Appendix I

ASPCA Chairmen or Equivalent

Henry Bergh	1866–1888
Henry Bergh Jr. (the founder's nephew)	1888–1889
John P. Haines	1889–1906
Alfred Wagstaff	1906–1921
Frank K. Sturgis	1921–1931
George M. Woolsey	1931–1937
Alexander S. Webb	1937–1947
John D. Beals, Jr.	1947–1952
Hugh E. Paine	1952–1955
William A. Rockefeller	1955–1963
James H. Jenkins	1963–1969
John F. Thompson Jr.	1969–1971
Charles S. Haines	1971–1973
Alastair B. Martin	1973–1976
Louis F. Bishop III	1976–1979
Marvin Schiller	1979–1981
George W. Gowen	1981–1983
Thomas N. McCarter III	1983–1995
James F. Stebbins	1995–1997
Steven M. Elkman	1997–2003
Hoyle C. Jones	2003–

ASPCA Presidents or Equivalent

Henry Bergh	1866–1888
N. P. Hosack	1868–1877

Thomas W. Hartfield	1873–1882
Charles H. Hankinson	1882–1907
William K. Horton	1907–1929
William E. Bevan	1929–1937
Eugene Berlinghoff	1935–1953
Warren W. McSpadden	1953–1958
Arthur L. Amundsen	1958–1961
William Mapel	1960–1972
Encil E. Rains	1972–1977
Duncan Wright	1977–1978
John F. Kullberg, Ed.D.	1978–1991
Roger A. Caras	1991–1998
Larry M. Hawk, D.V.M.	1999–2003
Edwin J. Sayres	2003–

Appendix II

ASPCA Canine Behavior Evaluation Form
Instructions for Use

1. Case number:
2. Evaluator: Name of individual performing the evaluation
3. Date: Date of the evaluation
4. Time: AM-morning PM-afternoon
5. Kennel Card Number: ASPCA entry number
6. Kennel: Kennel number
7. Date of entry: Day brought into the shelter
8. Sex: Sex of the animal
9. Age: Best estimate of age
10. Status: N - neutered
    S - spayed
    ? - unknown
    X - not spayed or neutered
    H - in heat
11. This must be filled out *before* doing behavior evaluation

   Breed: Pure - obvious purebred (may or may not have papers)
   mixed - obvious mix
   Description - breed if purebred; mix if mixed (i.e., terrier/hound) or pre-dominate type
   Breed types - based on AKC categories. Breed number to be assigned based on description above (i.e., collie, Dobie, poodle, etc.). If the dog is a mix try to assign a general grouping based on appearance, *not behavior*, as we are trying to see how well behavior conforms to appearance.

12. Behavior

   1. Sociability: When the dog is at the end of the leash, be solicitous to the dog: crouch, call in a high-pitched voice.

     5 - immediate response and stays to interact
     3 - several calls required; does not stay to interact
     1 - dog does not respond

   2. Dominance: How easy is it to get the dog into a sit with no verbal cue (i.e., one hand on dog's hips, one hand on collar).

     5 - dog turns on handler
     4 - active resistance (twists/turns)
     3 - passive resistance
     2 - slow response
     1 - readily responds

   3. Confidence: Based on observation outside of the kennel area; primarily based on postural cues.

     5 - tail up/ears up; relaxed; tail wag
     3 - mixed cues (i.e., tail up/ears down)
     1 - tail tucked; skittish; trembling; low posture

   4. Touch sensitivity: Based on subjective assessment of response to a toe-squeeze or rump-grasp.

   5. Sound sensitivity: Based on subjective response to ambient sounds during evaluation.

   6. Vocalization: In kennel and out during observation.

     5 - constant barking or whining
     3 - intermittent barking or whining
     1 - no evidence

   7. Mouth: Based on events during evaluation; i.e., during test for dominance; when placing the leash on the dog; when testing for touch sensitivity.

   8. Activity/vigor: Based on response to commands, play solicitation; walking, etc.

     5 - jumping, springs up, runs, dashes
     3 - participates with gusto; jaunty
     1 - lethargic, low enthusiasm

   9. Aggression/Human: By observation and/or provocation.

     5 - can't remove from the cage
     4 - apparently unprovoked attack when out of the cage

3 - strong display when provoked

2 - minimal display when provoked

1 - unable to provoke

10. Aggression/Dog: By observation while walking the dog.

5 - strong, persistent lunge or attack (outside of kennel area)

3 - display toward another dog

1 - no evidence

11. Leash: Based on experience while walking the dog.

5 - heels

3 - comfortable within radius of the leash

1 - fights the leash

Canine Behavior Evaluation Form[*]

Case number_____   AM

Evaluator_____ Date_____   PM

Kennel Card number_____   Kennel _____

Date of entry _____   Sex   M   F

Age   _____   Status   N   S   ?   X   H

Breed: pure ___ mixed ___ description_____

Breed types:

(10) Herding ___   (20) Hound   ___   (30) Non-Sporting ___

(40) Spitz   ___   (50) Sporting   ___   (60) Terrier   ___

(70) Toy   ___   (80) Working   ___   (90) Exotic   ___

(00) Undetermined mix   _____

Size:

(01) Large ____

(02) Medium ____

(03) Small ____

Behavior

1.	Sociability: aloof	1	2	3	4	5	social
2.	Dominance: submissive	1	2	3	4	5	pushy
3.	Confidence: terrified	1	2	3	4	5	bold
4.	Touch: insensitive	1	2	3	4	5	sensitive
5.	Sound: insensitive	1	2	3	4	5	sensitive
6.	Vocalization: none	1	2	3	4	5	constant
7.	Mouth: no use	1	2	3	4	5	nip/bite
8.	Activity/vigor: low	1	2	3	4	5	hyperactive
9.	Aggression/human: low	1	2	3	4	5	high
10.	Aggression/dog: low	1	2	3	4	4	high
11.	Leash: fights	1	2	3	4	5	heels

Adoption Guidelines:

Recommended Homes:

1. Any Home
2. Home with Children
3. Senior Citizens

4. Small Apartment
5. Home with Yard
6. High Activity (e.g., jogging)
7. Low Activity Home

Recommended Restrictions:

1. Supplemental Adoption Form Required
2. Bite Waiver Required
3. No Children
4. No Small Children
5. No Other Dogs
6. No Other Pets
7. Early Full Time Socialization

Other Comments:

*This is the original evaluation form used at the ASPCA shelter circa 1988. It is believed to represent the first formal evaluation of shelter dogs in the United States.

Appendix III

ASPCA Pet Books

Complete Cat Care Manual
Andrew Edney
Dorling Kindersley, Inc.
New York, NY
1992

Complete Dog Care Manual
Bruce Fogle, D.V.M.
Dorling Kindersley, Inc.
New York, NY
1993

ASPCA Complete Dog Training Manual
Bruce Fogle, D.V.M.
Dorling Kindersley, Inc.
New York, NY
1994

ASPCA Dog Training (paperback)
Bruce Fogle, D.V.M.
Dorling Kindersley, Inc.
New York, NY
1999

ASPCA Complete Guide to Cats
James R. Richards, D.V.M.
Chronicle Books
San Francisco, CA
1999

ASPCA Complete Guide to Dogs
Sheldon L. Gerstenfeld, V.M.D., with Jacque Lynn Schultz
Chronicle Books
San Francisco, CA
1999

Appendix IV

The 2000 ASPCA Henry Bergh Children's Book Award and Honor Winners

Non-Fiction Companion Animals:

Winner, 2000 ASPCA Henry Bergh Children's Book Award
Go Home: The True Story of James the Cat by Libby Phillips Meggs
Albert Whitman & Company

Non-Fiction Environment and Ecology:

Winner, 2000 ASPCA Henry Bergh Children's Book Award
The Orphan Seal by Fran Hodgkins
Down East Books

Winner, 2000 ASPCA Henry Bergh Children's Book Honor
The Everything Kids' Nature Book by Kathiann M. Kowalski
Adams Media Corporation

Non-Fiction Humane Heroes:

Winner, 2000 ASPCA Henry Bergh Children's Book Award
John Muir: My Life With Nature by Joseph Cornell
Dawn Publications

Fiction Companion Animals:

Winner, 2000 ASPCA Henry Bergh Children's Book Award
Star in the Storm by Joan Hiatt Harlow
Simon & Schuster Children's Publishing Division

Fiction Environment and Ecology:

Winner, 2000 ASPCA Henry Bergh Children's Book Honor
The Spirit of the Masai Man by Laura Berkeley
Barefoot Books

Fiction Humane Heroes:

Winner, 2000 ASPCA Henry Bergh Children's Book Award
Fight for Life: Wild at Heart Book #1 by Laurie Halse Anderson
Pleasant Company

Poetry:

Winner, 2000 ASPCA Henry Bergh Children's Book Award
Each Living Thing by Joanne Ryder
Harcourt

Winner, 2000 ASPCA Henry Bergh Children's Book Honor
It's About Dogs by Tony Johnston
Harcourt

The 2001 ASPCA Henry Bergh Children's Book Award and Honor Winners

Non-Fiction Companion Animals:

Winner, 2001 ASPCA Henry Bergh Children's Book Award
Gold Rush Dogs by Claire Rudolf Murphy and Jane G. Haigh
Alaska Northwest Books

Winner, 2001 ASPCA Henry Bergh Children's Book Honor
AnimalWays Horses by Rebecca Stefoff
Benchmark Books, Marshall Cavendish

Non-Fiction Environment and Ecology:

Winner, 2001 ASPCA Henry Bergh Children's Book Award
Interrupted Journey by Kathryn Lasky
Candlewick Press

Non-Fiction Humane Heroes:

Winner, 2001 ASPCA Henry Bergh Children's Book Award
The Chimpanzees I Love: Saving Their World and Ours by Jane Goodall
Scholastic Press, A Byron Preiss Book

Winner, 2001 ASPCA Henry Bergh Children's Book Honor
Pets to the Rescue: Brave Norman—A True Story by Andrew Clements
Simon & Schuster Children's Publishing

Fiction Companion Animals:

Winner, 2001 ASPCA Henry Bergh Children's Book Award
One Unhappy Horse by C. S. Adler
Clarion Books

Winner, 2001 ASPCA Henry Bergh Children's Book Honor
"Let's Get a Pup!" Said Kate by Bob Graham
Candlewick Press

Fiction Environment and Ecology:

Winner, 2001 ASPCA Henry Bergh Children's Book Honor
Jubela by Cristina Kessler
Simon & Schuster Children's Publishing

Winner, 2001 ASPCA Henry Bergh Children's Book Honor
Bears Barge In by Joni Sensel
Dream Factory Books

Fiction Humane Heroes:

Winner, 2001 ASPCA Henry Bergh Children's Book Award
Saving Lilly by Peg Kehret
Simon & Schuster Children's Publishing

Poetry:

Winner, 2001 ASPCA Henry Bergh Children's Book Honor
Leap into Poetry: More ABC's of Poetry by Avis Harley
Boyds Mills Press

The 2002 ASPCA Henry Bergh Children's Book Award and Honor Winners

Non-Fiction Companion Animals:

Winner, 2002 ASPCA Henry Bergh Children's Book Award
A Kid's Best Friend by Maya Ajmera and Alex Fisher
Charlesbridge Publishing

Winner, 2002 ASPCA Henry Bergh Children's Book Honor
Cherry Hill's Horse Care for Kids by Cherry Hill
Storey Kids/Storey Books

Non-Fiction Environment and Ecology:

Winner, 2002 ASPCA Henry Bergh Children's Book Award
Animal Talk: How Animals Communicate Through Sight, Sound and Smell by
    Etta Kaner
Kids Can Press, Ltd.

Non-Fiction Humane Heroes:

Winner, 2002 ASPCA Henry Bergh Children's Book Award
The Elephant Hospital by Kathy Darling
The Millbrook Press, Inc.

Fiction Companion Animals:

Winner, 2002 ASPCA Henry Bergh Children's Book Award
Jasper's Day by Marjorie Blain Parker
Kids Can Press, Ltd.

Winner, 2002 ASPCA Henry Bergh Children's Book Honor
Stray Dog by Kathe Koja
Farrar, Straus & Giroux

Fiction Environment and Ecology:

Winner, 2002 ASPCA Henry Bergh Children's Book Award
Goose's Story by Cari Best
Farrar, Straus & Giroux

Fiction Humane Heroes:

Winner, 2002 ASPCA Henry Bergh Children's Book Honor
Little Flower by Gloria Rand
Henry Holt & Company

Winner, 2002 ASPCA Henry Bergh Children's Book Honor
Monkey for Sale by Sanna Stanley
Farrar, Straus & Giroux

Poetry:

Winner, 2002 ASPCA Henry Bergh Children's Book Award
The Turtle Saver by Laurie Parker
Quail Ridge Press

Illustration:

Winner, 2002 ASPCA Henry Bergh Children's Illustration Award
Jasper's Day by Marjorie Blain Parker, illustrated by Janet Wilson
Kids Can Press, Ltd.

The 2003 ASPCA Henry Bergh Children's Book Award and Honor Winners

Non-Fiction Companion Animals:

Winner, 2003 ASPCA Henry Bergh Children's Book Award
Working Like a Dog: The Story of Working Dogs Through History by Gena
 K. Gorrell
Tundra Books

Non-Fiction Environment and Ecology:

Winner, 2003 ASPCA Henry Bergh Children's Book Award
Safari Journal by Hudson Talbott
Harcourt

Winner, 2003 ASPCA Henry Bergh Children's Book Honor
Buffalo: With Selections from Native American Song Poems by Beverly
 Brodsky
Marshall Cavendish

Non-Fiction Humane Heroes:

Winner, 2003 ASPCA Henry Bergh Children's Book Award
Freckles: The Mystery of the Little White Dog in the Desert by Paul M.
 Howey
AZTexts Publishing

Winner, 2003 ASPCA Henry Bergh Children's Book Honor
Wild Horses: Black Hills Sanctuary by Cris Peterson
Boyds Mills Press

Fiction Environment and Ecology:

Winner, 2003 ASPCA Henry Bergh Children's Book Award
The Deliverance of Dancing Bears by Elizabeth Stanley
Kane/Miller Book Publishers

Fiction Humane Heroes:

Winner, 2003 ASPCA Henry Bergh Children's Book Award
Seldovia Sam and the Sea Otter Rescue by Susan Woodward Springer
Alaska Northwest Books

Winner, 2003 ASPCA Henry Bergh Children's Book Honor
In Flanders Fields by Norman Jorgensen
Simply Read Books

Poetry:

Winner, 2003 ASPCA Henry Bergh Children's Book Award
The World According to Dog: Poems and Teen Voices by Joyce Sidman
Houghton Mifflin Company

Winner, 2003 ASPCA Henry Bergh Children's Book Honor
Swan Song: Poems of Extinction by J. Patrick Lewis
The Creative Company

Illustration:

Winner, 2003 ASPCA Henry Bergh Children's Illustration Award
The Deliverance of Dancing Bears by Elizabeth Stanley
Kane/Miller Book Publishers

The 2004 ASPCA Henry Bergh Children's Book Award and Honor Winners

Non-Fiction Companion Animals:

Winner, 2004 ASPCA Henry Bergh Children's Book Honor
Hachiko: The True Story of a Loyal Dog by Pamela Turner
Houghton Mifflin Company

Non-Fiction Environment and Ecology:

Winner, 2004 ASPCA Henry Bergh Children's Book Award
Tree of Life: The Incredible Biodiversity of Life on Earth by Rochelle Strauss
Kids Can Press, Ltd.

Winner, 2004 ASPCA Henry Bergh Children's Book Honor
Changing the Future for Endangered Wildlife Series
Chimpanzee Rescue by Patricia Bow

Frog Rescue by Garry Hamilton
Elephant Rescue by Jody Morgan
Firefly Books, Ltd.

Non-Fiction Humane Heroes:

Winner, 2004 ASPCA Henry Bergh Children's Book Award
The Goat Lady by Jane Bregoli
Tilbury House, Publishers

Fiction Companion Animals:

Winner, 2004 ASPCA Henry Bergh Children's Book Award
Saying Goodbye to Lulu by Corinne Demas
Little, Brown and Company Books for Young Readers

Winner, 2004 ASPCA Henry Bergh Children's Book Honor
Hachiko Waits by Lesléa Newman
Henry Holt and Company

Fiction Environment and Ecology:

Winner, 2004 ASPCA Henry Bergh Children's Book Award
Pinduli by Janell Cannon
Harcourt

Poetry:

Winner, 2004 ASPCA Henry Bergh Children's Book Award
Hummingbird Nest: A Journal of Poems by Kristine O'Connell George
Harcourt

Young Adult:

Winner, 2004 ASPCA Henry Bergh Young Adult Award
Our Secret, Siri Aang by Cristina Kessler
Philomel Books division of Penguin Young Readers Group

Illustration:

Winner, 2004 ASPCA Henry Bergh Children's Illustration Award
Animals Asleep by Sneed B. Collard III, illustrated by Anik McGrory
Houghton Mifflin Company

The 2005 ASPCA Henry Bergh Children's Book Award and Honor Winners

Non-Fiction Companion Animals:

Winner, 2005 ASPCA Henry Bergh Children's Book Award
Tails Are Not for Pulling (set) by Elizabeth Verdick
Free Spirit Publishing

Winner, 2005 ASPCA Henry Bergh Children's Book Honor
ER Vets: Life in an Animal Emergency Room by Donna M. Jackson
Houghton Mifflin Company

Non-Fiction Environment and Ecology:

Winner, 2005 ASPCA Henry Bergh Children's Book Award
Scientists in the Field series:
Gorilla Doctors: Saving Endangered Great Apes by Pamela S. Turner
The Prairie Builders by Sneed B. Collard III
Houghton Mifflin Company

Non-Fiction Humane Heroes:

Winner, 2005 ASPCA Henry Bergh Children's Book Award
The Least of These by Joan Harris
West Winds Press

Fiction Companion Animals:

Winner, 2005 ASPCA Henry Bergh Children's Book Award
Dog Sense by Sneed B. Collard III
Peachtree

Winner, 2005 ASPCA Henry Bergh Children's Book Award
A Dog's Life: The Autobiography of a Stray by Ann M. Martin
Scholastic

Fiction Environment and Ecology:

Winner, 2005 ASPCA Henry Bergh Children's Book Award
And Tango Makes Three by Justin Richardson and Peter Parnell
Simon & Schuster

Fiction Humane Heroes:

Winner, 2005 ASPCA Henry Bergh Children's Book Award
Magnus at the Fire by Jennifer Armstrong
Simon & Schuster

Poetry:

Winner, 2005 ASPCA Henry Bergh Children's Book Award
So What's It Like to Be a Cat? by Karla Kuskin
Simon & Schuster

Young Adult:

Winner, 2005 ASPCA Henry Bergh Young Adult Award
Defiance by Valerie Hobbs
Farrar, Straus and Giroux

Illustration:

Winner, 2005 ASPCA Henry Bergh Illustration Award
Earth Mother by Ellen Jackson, illustrated by Leo and Diane Dillon
Walker & Company

Winner, 2005 ASPCA Henry Bergh Illustration Honor
Cool Time Song by Carole Lexa Schaefer, illustrated by Pierr Morgan
Penguin Putnam

The 2006 ASPCA Henry Bergh Children's Book Award and Honor Winners

Non-Fiction Companion Animals:

Winner, 2006 ASPCA Henry Bergh Children's Book Award
Is My Dog a Wolf? by Jenni Bidner
Lark Books/Sterling Publishing

Non-Fiction Environment and Ecology:

Winner, 2006 ASPCA Henry Bergh Children's Book Award
Quest for the Tree Kangaroo by Sy Montgomery
Houghton Mifflin Company

Non-Fiction Humane Heroes:

Winner, 2006 ASPCA Henry Bergh Children's Book Award
Dog Heroes Series
Water Rescue Dogs by Frances E. Ruffin
Fire Dogs by Donna Latham
Bearport Publishing

Fiction Companion Animals:

Winner, 2006 ASPCA Henry Bergh Children's Book Award
Buddy Unchained by Daisy Bix
Gryphon Press

Fiction Environment and Ecology:

Winner, 2006 ASPCA Henry Bergh Children's Book Award
Tale of a Great White Fish by Maggie De Vries
Greystone Books/Douglas & McIntyre

Fiction Humane Heroes:

Winner, 2006 ASPCA Henry Bergh Children's Book Award
Wings by William Loizeaux
Farrar, Straus & Giroux

Poetry:

Winner, 2006 ASPCA Henry Bergh Children's Book Award
Butterfly Eyes and Other Secrets of the Meadow by Joyce Sidman
Houghton Mifflin Company

Young Adult:

Winner, 2006 ASPCA Henry Bergh Young Adult Award
One Kingdom: Our Lives with Animals by Deborah Noyes
Houghton Mifflin Company

Winner, 2006 ASPCA Henry Bergh Young Adult Award
Listen! by Stephanie S. Tolan
Harper Collins

Winner, 2006 ASPCA Henry Bergh Young Adult Honor
Flash Point by Sneed B. Collard III
Peachtree Publishers

Illustration:

Winner, 2006 ASPCA Henry Bergh Illustration Award
Butterfly Eyes and Other Secrets of the Meadow by Joyce Sidman, illustrated
   by Beth Krommes
Houghton Mifflin Company

Appendix V

The Asilomar Accords[*]

Preface

In August of 2004, a group of animal welfare industry leaders from across the nation convened at Asilomar in Pacific Grove, California, for the purpose of building bridges across varying philosophies, developing relationships and creating goals focused on significantly reducing the euthanasia of healthy and treatable companion animals in the United States. Through hard work, lively discussion and brainstorming, a common vision for the future was adopted. The leadership of twenty organizations participated in the original, and/or subsequent meetings and were involved in the drafting of the "Asilomar Accords."

Guiding Principles

1. The mission of those involved in creating the *Asilomar Accords* is to work together to save the lives of all healthy and treatable companion animals.
2. We recognize that all stakeholders in the animal welfare community have a passion for and are dedicated to the mutual goal of saving animals' lives.
3. We acknowledge that the euthanasia of healthy and treatable animals is the sad responsibility of some animal welfare organizations that neither desired nor sought this task. We believe that the euthanasia of healthy and treatable animals is a community-wide problem requiring community-based solutions. We also recognize that animal welfare organizations can be leaders in bringing about a change in social order and other factors that result in the euthanasia of healthy and treatable animals, including the compounding problems of some pet owners'/guardians' failure to spay and neuter, properly socialize and train; be tolerant of; provide veterinary care to; or take responsibility for companion animals.

169

4. We, as animal welfare stakeholders, agree to foster a mutual respect for one another. When discussing differences of policy and opinion, either publicly or within and among our own agencies, we agree to refrain from denigrating or speaking ill of one another. We will also encourage those other individuals and organizations in our sphere of influence to do the same.

5. We encourage all communities to embrace the vision and spirit of these Accords, while acknowledging that differences exist between various communities and geographic regions of the country.

6. We encourage the creation of local "community coalitions" consisting of a variety of organizations (e.g., governmental animal control agencies, nonprofit shelters, grassroots foster care providers, feral cat groups, funders and veterinary associations) for the purpose of saving the lives of healthy and treatable animals. We are committed to the belief that no one organization or type of organization can achieve this goal alone, and that we need one another, and that the only true solution is to work together. We need to find common ground, put aside our differences and work collaboratively to reach the ultimate goal of ending the euthanasia of healthy and treatable companion animals.

7. While we understand that other types of programs and efforts (including adoption, spay and neuter programs, education, cruelty investigations, enforcement of animal control laws and regulation, behavior and training assistance and feral cat management) play a critical role in impacting euthanasia figures, for purposes of this nationwide initiative we have elected to leave these programs in the hands of local organizations and encourage them to continue offering, and expanding upon, these critical services.

8. In order to achieve harmony and forward progress, we encourage each community coalition to discuss language and terminology which has been historically viewed as hurtful or divisive by some animal welfare stakeholders (whether intentional or inadvertent), identify "problem" language, and reach a consensus to modify or phase out language and terminology accordingly.

9. We believe in the importance of transparency and the open sharing of accurate, complete animal sheltering data and statistics in a manner which is clear to both the animal welfare community and the public.

10. We believe it is essential to utilize a uniform method of collecting and reporting shelter data, in order to promote transparency and better assess the euthanasia rate of healthy and treatable animals. We determined that uniform method of reporting needs to include the collection and analysis of animal-sheltering data as set forth in the "Animal Statistics Table." These statistics need to be collected for each individual organization and for the community as a whole and need to be reported to the public annually (e.g., web sites, newsletters, annual reports). In addition, we

determined that each community's "Live Release Rate" needs to be cal-
culated, shared and reported annually to the public, individually by each
organization and jointly by each community coalition. Both individual
organizations and community coalitions should strive for continuous
improvement of these numbers. The "Animal Statistics Table" and formulas for calculating the "Live Release Rate" are set forth in Section IV
of these Accords.

11. We developed several standard "definitions" to enable uniform and accurate collection, analysis and reporting of animal-sheltering data and statistics. We encourage all communities to adopt the definitions which are set
forth in Section III, and implement the principles of these Accords.

12. While we recognize that many animal welfare organizations provide services to companion animals other than dogs and cats, for purposes of this
nationwide initiative we have elected to collect and share data solely as it
relates to dogs and cats.

13. We are committed to continuing dialogue, analysis and potential modification of this vision as needs change and as progress is made toward
achieving our mission.

14. Those involved in the development of the *Asilomar Accords* have agreed to
make a personal commitment to ensure the futherance of these accords,
and to use their professional influence to bring about nationwide adoption
of this vision.

Definitions

In order to facilitate the data collection process and assure consistent
reporting across agencies, the following definitions have been developed.
The Asilomar participants hope that these definitions are applied as a
standard for categorizing dogs and cats in each organization. The definitions, however, are not meant to define the outcome for each animal
entrusted to our care.

Healthy. The term "healthy" means and includes all dogs and cats
eight weeks of age or older that, at or subsequent to the time the animal
is taken into possession, have manifested no sign of a behavioral or
temperamental characteristic that could pose a health or safety risk or otherwise make the animal unsuitable for placement as a pet, and have manifested no sign of disease, injury, a congenital or hereditary condition that
adversely affects the heat of the animal or that is likely to aversely affect
the animal's health in the future.

Treatable. The term "treatable" means and includes all dogs and cats
who are "rehabilitatable" and all dogs and cats who are "manageable."

Rehabilitatable: The term "rehabilitatable" means and includes all
dogs and cats who are not "healthy," but are likely to become "healthy,"

if given medical, foster, behavioral, or other care equivalent to the care typically provided to pets by reasonable and caring pet owners/guardians in the community.

Manageable: The term "manageable" means and includes all dogs and cats who are not "healthy" and who are not likely to become "healthy," regardless of the care provided; but who would likely maintain a satisfactory quality of life, if given medical, foster, behavioral, or other care, including long-term care, equivalent to the care typically provided to pets by reasonable and caring owners/guardians in the community; provided, however, that the term "manageable" does not include any dog or cat who is determined to pose a significant risk to human health or safety or to the health or safety of other animals.

Unhealthy and Untreatable. The term "unhealthy and untreatable" means and includes all dogs and cats who, at or subsequent to the time they are taken into possession:

1. have a behavioral or temperamental characteristic that poses a health or safety risk or otherwise makes the animal unsuitable for placement as a pet, and are not likely to become "healthy" or "treatable" even if provided the care typically provided to pets by reasonable and caring pet owner/guardians in the community; or
2. are suffering from a disease, injury or congenital or hereditary condition that adversely affects the animal's health or is likely to adversely affect the animal's health in the future, and are not likely to become "healthy" or "treatable" even if provided the care typically provided to pets by reasonable and caring pet/guardians in the community; or
3. are under the age of eight weeks and are not likely to become "healthy" or "treatable," even if provided the care typically provided to pets by reasonable and care pet owners/guardians in the community.

---

*Excerpted from the "Asilomar Accords" document.

Appendix VI

Berghliography: Books about Henry Bergh and the ASPCA

Alexander, Lloyd. *Fifty Years in the Doghouse: The Adventures of William Michael Ryan, Special Agent No. 1 of the ASPCA*. New York: G. P. Putnam's Sons, 1963.

Beers, Diane L. *For the Prevention of Cruelty: The History and Legacy of Animal Rights Activism in the United States*. Athens, OH: Swallow Press/University of Ohio Press, 2006.

Bekoff, Marc A. *Encyclopedia of Animal Rights and Animal Welfare*. Westport, CT: Greenwood Press, 1998.

Carlson, Gerald. *Men, Beasts, and Gods: A History of Cruelty and Kindness to Animals*. New York: Charles Scribner's Sons, 1972. (Chapter 10)

Coleman, Sydney H. *Humane Society Leaders in America: With a Sketch of the Early History of the Movement in England*. Albany, NY: American Humane Association, 1924. (Chapters II and III)

Coren, Stanley. *The Pawprints of History: Dogs and the Course of Human Events*. New York: Free Press, 2002. (Chapter 13)

Harlow, Alvin F. *Henry Bergh—Founder of the A.S.P.C.A.* New York: Julian Messner, 1957.

Hoff, Sid. *The Man Who Loved Animals*. New York: Coward, McCann & Geoghegan, Inc., 1982.

Loeper, John J. *Crusade for Kindness: Henry Bergh and the ASPCA*. New York: Atheneum, 1991.

Pace, Mildred Mastin. *Friend of Animals: The Story of Henry Bergh*. Ashland, KY: The Jesse Stuart Foundation, 1995.

Shelman, Eric A., and Stephen Lazoritz. *Out of the Darkness: The Story of Mary Ellen Wilson*. Lake Forest, CA: Dolphin Moon Publishing, 1998.

Steele, Zulma. *Angel in Top Hat*. New York: Harper & Brothers, 1942.

Turner, James. *Reckoning with the Beast*. Baltimore, MD: Johns Hopkins University Press, 1980.

Unti, Bernard Oreste. *The Quality of Mercy: Organized Animal Protection in the United States 1866–1930*. Diss. American University, 2002.

Bibliography

Alexander, Lloyd. *Fifty Years in the Doghouse*. New York: G. P. Putnam's Sons, 1963.

Buffet, Edward P. "Bergh's War on Vested Cruelty," unpublished manuscript. New York, NY: ASPCA Archives, Undated.

Grier, Katherine C. *Pets in America: A History*. Chapel Hill: University of North Carolina Press, 2006.

Hurley, Kate, and Lila Miller. *Management of Infectious Diseases in Animal Shelters*. Ames, IA: Blackwell Publishing, 2008.

Martin, Edward C., Jr. *Dr. Johnson's Apple Orchard: The Story of America's First Pet Cemetery*. New York: Hartsdale Canine Cemetery, 1997.

Merck, Melinda. *Veterinary Forensics: Animal Cruelty Investigations*. Ames, IA: Blackwell Publishing, 2007.

Miller, Lila, and Stephen Zawistowski. *Shelter Medicine for Veterinarians and Staff*. Ames, IA: Blackwell Publishing, 2004.

Reid, Pamela J. *Excel-Erated Learning: Explaining in Plain English How Dogs Learn and How Best to Teach Them*. Berkeley, CA: James & Kenneth Publishers, 1996.

Saunders, Blanche. *The Complete Book of Dog Obedience: A Guide for Trainers* (New expanded edition). New York: Howell Book House, 1978.

Saunders, Blanche, and Catharine Conway Reiley. *The Story of Dog Obedience*. New York: Howell Book House, 1974.

Schultz, William J. *The Humane Movement in the United States, 1910–1922*. New York: Columbia University Press, 1924.

Scott, John Paul, and John L. Fuller. *Genetics and the Social Behavior of Dogs* (Reprint paperback edition). Chicago, IL: University of Chicago Press, 1998.

Shapiro, Kenneth J., and Stephen L. Zawistowski, eds. *Journal of Applied Animal Welfare Science,* Vols. 1–10. Mahwah, NJ: Lawrence Erlbaum Associates, 1998–2007.

Szasz, Kathleen. *Petishism: Pets and Their People in the Western World*. Austin, TX: Holt, Rinehart and Winston, 1969.

Zawistowski, Stephen. *Companion Animals in Society*. Clifton Park, NY: Thomson Delmar Learning, 2008.

Index

About the Authors

MARION S. LANE is Special Projects Editor in the National Program Office of the American Society for the Prevention of Cruelty to Animals. The former editor of *ASPCA Animal Watch* and *Pure-Bred Dogs/American Kennel Gazette*, she has written dozens of personal essays and feature articles on pets as well as four nonfiction books on dogs. She is the recipient of awards for both writing and editing from the Dog Writers Association of America, the Society of National Association Publications and folio: magazine.

STEPHEN L. ZAWISTOWSKI is Executive Vice President and Science Advisor of the American Society for the Prevention of Cruelty to Animals, where he currently oversees the ASPCA's National Programs. "Dr. Z." is a certified applied animal behaviorist who chairs the Animal Behavior Society's Board of Professional Certification and is a frequent speaker on animal behavior, the history of sheltering, humane education, and the use of statistics in program management. A founding editor of the *Journal of Applied Animal Welfare Science*, adjunct professor of clinical medicine at the University of Illinois College of Veterinary Medicine, and member of National Academy of Sciences–National Research Council Committees to review the National Zoo and revise guidelines on distress in laboratory animals, he also co-edited *Shelter Medicine for Veterinarians and Staff*.